Classic English Love Poems

Classic English Love Poems

Edited by
Emile Capouya

HIPPOCRENE BOOKS
New York

For information, address:
HIPPOCRENE BOOKS, INC.
171 Madison Avenue
New York, NY 10016

Library of Congress Cataloging-in-Publication Data
Classic English love poems / edited by Emile Capouya.
    p.   cm
    ISBN 0-7818-0572-4
    1. Love poetry, English. I. Capouya, Emile
PR1184.C714   1998
821.008'03543—dc21   97-24432
                                                 CIP

Printed in the United States of America.

Contents

Foreword

This collection begins in the fourteenth century and ends in the first third of the twentieth. The reader will find that the literature of love in England is an era in itself. In these pages are the art and countenance of a nation—more, a world-wide treasure wherever English is spoken.

The verses here span six hundred years, and might have blossomed still, but the First World War, with its heroism, and its horrors, changed the planet, in manners, expectations, morals, philosophies, and thought.

Robert Mannyng, or Robert de Brunne (1288-1338)

> No thyng is to man so dere
> As wommanys love in gode manere.
> A gode womman is manny blys,
> There here love right and stedfast is.

Alfred Edward Housman (1859-1936)

> "Is my friend hearty,
> Now I am thin and pine,
> And has he found to sleep in
> A better bed than mine?"
>
> Yes, lad, I lie easy,
> I lie as lads would choose;
> I cheer a dead man's sweetheart,
> Never ask me whose.

These lines above, taken from the originals, suggest the temper of the long flow of discoveries in English poetry, often imported from other languages. At its height it was a marvel.

With its passing, rhyme was abandoned. That special music is now very rare.

—- Emile Capouya

Classic English Love Poems

ROBERT MANNYNG OF BRUNNE
1288-1338

Praise of Women

No thyng is to man so dere
As wommanys love in gode manere.
A gode womman is mannys blys,
There here love right and stedfast is.
There is no solas under hevene,
Of alle that a man may nevene[1],
That shuld a man do so moche glew[2]
As a gode womman that loveth trew.
Ne derer is none in Goddys hurde[3]
Than a chaste womman with lovely worde.

[1]name
[2]gladness.
[3]flock.

GEOFFREY CHAUCER
?1343-1400

Balade

Hide, Absalom, thy gilté tresses clear;
 Esther, lay thou thy meekness all a-down;
Hide, Jonathan, all thy friendly mannér;
 Penelope and Marcia Catóun
 Make of your wifehood no comparisón;
 Hide ye your beauties, Isolde and Elaine:
 My lady com'th, that all this may distain.

Thy fairé body let it not appear,
 Lavine; and thou, Lucrece of Romé town,
And Polixene, that boughten love so dear,
 And Cleopatre, with all thy passión,
 Hide ye your truth of love and your renown;
 And thou, Thisbe, that hast for love such pain:
 My lady com'th, that all this may distain.

Hero, Dido, Laodámia, all y-fere,
 And Phyllis, hanging for thy Demophon,
And Cánacé, espièd by thy chere,
 Hypsípylé, betraysèd with Jasón,
 Make of your truthé neither boast ne soun;
 Nor Hypermestre or Ariadne, ye twain:
 My lady com'th, that all this may distain.

CHARLES OF ORLEANS
?1394-1465

A Lover's Confession

My ghostly father, I me confess,
  First to God and then to you,
  That at a window—wot ye how?
I stole a kiss of great sweetness,
Which done was out avisedness[1];
  But it is done, not undone, now.
My ghostly father, I me confess,
  First to God and then to you.
But I restore it shall doubtless
  Again, if so be that I mow;
  And that to God I make avow,
And else I ask forgiveness.
My ghostly father, I me confess,
  First to God and then to you,
  That at a window—wot ye how?
I stole a kiss of great sweetness.

[1]without thought

17

ANONYMOUS
c. 1500

Western Wind

Western Wind, when will thou blow,
    The small rain down can rain?
Christ, if my love were in my arms
    And I in my bed again!

SIR THOMAS WYATT
c. 1503-1542

Remembrance

They flee from me, that sometime did me seek
  With naked foot, stalking in my chamber.
I have seen them gentle, tame, and meek,
    That now are wild, and do not remember
    That sometime they put themselves in danger
      To take bread at my hand; and now they range
      Busily seeking with a continual change.

Thanked be fortune it hath been otherwise
  Twenty times better; but once, in special,
In thin array, after a pleasant guise,
    When her loose gown from her shoulders did fall,
    And she me caught in her arms long and small,
      Therewith all sweetly did me kiss
      And softly said, 'Dear heart, how like you this?'

It was no dream; I lay broad waking:
  But all is turned, thorough my gentleness,
Into a strange fashion of forsaking;
    And I have leave to go of her goodness,
    And she also to use newfangleness.
      But since that I so kindly am served,
      I would fain know what she hath deserved.

SIR PHILIP SIDNEY
1554-1586

The Bargain

My true love hath my heart, and I have his,
  By just exchange, one for the other given.
I hold his dear, and mine he cannot miss,
  There never was a better bargain driven.
His heart in me keeps me and him in one,
  My heart in him his thoughts and senses guides;
He loves my heart, for once it was his own,
  I cherish his, because in me it bides.
His heart his wound receivèd from my sight,
  My heart was wounded with his wounded heart;
For as from me on him his hurt did light,
  So still methought in me his hurt did smart.
    Both equal hurt, in this change sought our bliss:
    My true love hath my heart and I have his.

To the Sad Moon

With how sad steps, O Moon, thou climb'st the skies!
  How silently, and with how wan a face!
  What! may it be that even in heavenly place
That busy archer his sharp arrows tries?
Sure, if that long-with-love-acquainted eyes
  Can judge of love, thou feel'st a lover's case:
  I read it in thy looks; thy languished grace
To me, that feel the like, thy state descries.
Then, even of fellowship, O Moon, tell me,
  Is constant love deemed there but want of wit?

Are beauties there as proud as here they be?
　　Do they above love to be loved, and yet
　　　　Those lovers scorn whom that love doth possess?
　　　　Do they call 'virtue' there—ungratefulness?

JOHN LYLY
?1554-1606

Cards and Kisses

Cupid and my Campaspe played
At cards for kisses, Cupid paid;
He stakes his quiver, bow, and arrows,
His mother's doves, and team of sparrows;
Loses them too; then, down he throws
The coral of his lip, the rose
Growing on's cheek (but none knows how);
With these, the crystal of his brow,
And then the dimple of his chin:
All these did my Campaspe win.
At last, he set her both his eyes;
She won, and Cupid blind did rise.
    O Love! has she done this to thee?
    What shall (alas!) become of me?

WILLIAM SHAKESPEARE
1564-1616

Silvia

Who is Silvia? What is she?
　　That all our swains commend her?
Holy, fair, and wise is she;
　　The heaven such grace did lend her,
That she might admired be.

Is she kind as she is fair?
　　For beauty lives with kindness:
Love doth to her eyes repair,
　　To help him of his blindness;
And, being help'd, inhabits there.

Then to Silvia let us sing,
　　That Silvia is excelling;
She excels each mortal thing
　　Upon the dull earth dwelling:
To her let us garlands bring.

Feste's Songs

O Mistress mine, where are you roaming?
O! stay and hear; your true love's coming,
　　That can sing both high and low.
Trip no further, pretty sweeting;
Journeys end in lovers meeting,
　　Every wise man's son doth know.

What is love? 'Tis not hereafter;
Present mirth hath present laughter;
   What's to come is still unsure.
In delay there lies no plenty;
Then come kiss me, sweet and twenty;
   Youth's a stuff will not endure.

At the Moated Grange

Take, O! take those lips away,
   That so sweetly were forsworn,
And those eyes, the break of day,
   Lights that do mislead the morn;
But my kisses bring again,
     Bring again,
Seals of love, but sealed in vain,
     Sealed in vain.

Sonnets

(i)

Shall I compare thee to a summer's day?
   Thou art more lovely and more temperate:
Rough winds do shake the darling buds of May,
   And summer's lease hath all too short a date:
Sometime too hot the eye of heaven shines,
   And often is his gold complexion dimmed;
And every fair from fair sometime declines,
   By chance, or nature's changing course untrimmed;
But thy eternal summer shall not fade,
   Nor lose possession of that fair thou owest,
Nor shall death brag thou wanderest in his shade,

When in eternal lines to time thou growest;
   So long as men can breathe, or eyes can see,
   So long lives this, and this gives life to thee.

(ii)

When in disgrace with fortune and men's eyes
   I all alone beweep my outcast state,
And trouble deaf heaven with my bootless cries,
   And look upon myself, and curse my fate,
Wishing me like to one more rich in hope,
   Featured like him, like him with friends possessed,
Desiring this man's art, and that man's scope,
   With what I most enjoy contented least;
Yet in these thoughts myself almost despising,
   Haply I think on thee, and then my state,
Like to the lark at break of day arising
   From sullen earth, sings humns at heaven's gate;
     For thy sweet love remembered such wealth brings
     That then I scorn to change my state with kings.

(x)

That time of year thou mayst in me behold
   When yellow leaves, or none, or few, do hang
Upon those boughs which shake against the cold,
   Bare ruined choirs, where late the sweet birds sang.
In me thou seest the twilight of such day
   As after sunset fadeth in the west;
Which by and by black night doth take away,
   Death's second self, that seals up all in rest.
In me thou seest the glowing of such fire,
   That on the ashes of his youth doth lie,

As the death-bed whereon it must expire,
   Consumed with that which it was nourished by.
     This thou perceiv'st, which makes thy love more strong,
     To love that well which thou must leave ere long.

(xviii)

Let me not to the marriage of true minds
   Admit impediments. Love is not love
Which alters when it alteration finds,
   Or bends with the remover to remove.
O, no! it is an ever-fixed mark,
   That looks on tempess and is never shaken;
It is the star to every wandering bark,
   Whose worth's unknown, although his height be taken.
Love's not Time's fool, though rosy lips and cheeks
   Within his bending sickle's compass come;
Love alters not with his brief hours and weeks,
   But bears it out even to the edge of doom.
     If this be error, and upon me proved,
     I never writ, nor no man ever loved.

BEN JONSON
?1573-1637

Song—To Celia

Come my Celia, let us prove,
While wee may, the sports of love;
Time will not be ours for ever:
He, at length, our good will sever.
Spend not then his gifts in vaine.
Sunnes that set, may rise againe:
But, if once wee lose this light,
'Tis, with us, perpetuall night.
Why should we deferre our joyes?
Fame, and rumor are but toyes.
Cannot we delude they eyes
Of a few poore houshold spyes?
Or his easier eares beguile,
So removed by our wile?
'Tis no sinne, loves fruit to steale,
But the sweet theft to reveale:
To bee taken, to be seene,
These have crimes accounted beene.

To Celia

Drink to me only with thine eyes,
  And I will pledge with mine;
Or leave a kiss but in the cup
  And I'll not look for wine.
The thirst that from the soul doth rise
  Doth ask a drink divine;

BEN JONSON

But might I of Jove's nectar sup,
   I would not change for thine.

I sent thee late a rosy wreath,
   Not so much honouring thee
As giving it a hope that there
   It could not withered be;
But thou thereon didst only breathe,
   And sent'st it back to me;
Since when it grows, and smells, I swear,
   Not of itself but thee!

CHRISTOPHER MARLOWE
1564-1593

The Passionate Shepherd to His Love

Come live with me and be my love,
And we will all the pleasures prove,
That hills and valleys, dales and fields,
And all the craggy mountains yields.

There we will sit upon the rocks,
And see the shepherds feed their flocks,
By shallow rivers to whose falls
Melodious birds sing madrigals.

And I will make thee beds of roses
With a thousand fragrant posies,
A cap of flowers, and a kirtle
Embroidered all with leaves of myrtle;

A gown made of the finest wool
Whick from our pretty lambs we pull;
Fair lined slippers for the cold,
With buckles of the purest gold;

A belt of straw and ivy buds,
With coral clasps and amber studs:
And if these pleasures may thee move,
Come live with me and be my love.

The shepherd's swains shall dance and sing
For thy delight each May morning:
If these delights thy mind may move,
Then live with me and be my love.

SIR WALTER RALEGH
?1552-1618

The Nymph's Reply to the Shepherd

If all the world and love were young,
And truth in every shepherd's tongue,
These pretty pleasures might me move
To live with thee and be thy love.

Time drives the flocks from field to fold,
When rivers rage and rocks grow cold,
And Philomel becometh dumb;
The rest complains of cares to come.

The flowers do fade, and wanton fields
To wayward winter reckoning yields;
A honey tongue, a heart of gall,
Is fancy's spring, but sorrow's fall.

Thy gowns, thy shoes, thy beds of roses,
Thy cap, thy kirtle, and thy posies
Soon break, soon wither, soon forgotten,
In folly ripe, in reason rotten.

Thy belt of straw and ivy buds,
Thy coral clasps and amber studs,
All these in me no means can move
To come to thee and be thy love.

But could youth last and love still breed,
Had joys no date nor age no need,
Then these delights my mind might move
To live with thee and be thy love.

JOHN DONNE
1573-1631

The Good-morrow

I wonder by my troth, what thou, and I
Did, till we lov'd? were we not wean'd till then?
But suck'd on countrey pleasures, childishly?
Or snorted we in the seaven sleepers den?
T'was so; But this, all pleasures fancise bee.
If ever any beauty I did see,
Which I desir'd, and got, t'was but a dreame of thee.

And now good morrow to our waking soules,
Which watch not one another out of feare;
For love, all love of other sights controules,
And makes one little roome, an every where.
Let sea-discoverers to new worlds have gone,
Let Maps to others, worlds on worlds have showne,
Let us possesse one world, each hath one, and is one.

My face in thine eye, thine in mine appeares,
And true plaine hearst doe in the faces rest,
Where can we finde two better hemispheares
Without sharpe North, without declining West?
What ever dies, was not mixt equally;
If our two loves be one, or, thou and I
Love so alike, that none doe slacken, none can die.

The Canonization

For Godsake hold your tongue, and let me love,
    Or chide my palsie, or my gout,
My five gray haires, or ruin'd fortune flout,
      With wealth your state, your minde with Arts improve,
        Take you a course, get you a place,
        Observe his honour, or his grace,
Or the Kings reall, or his stamped face
    Comtemplate, what you will, approve,
    So you will let me love.

Alas, alas, who's injur'd by my love?
    What merchants ships have my sighs drown'd?
Who saies my teares have overflow'd his ground?
      When did my colds a forward spring remove?
        When did the heats which my veines fill
        Adde one more to the plaguie Bill?
Soldiers finde warres, and Lawyers finde out still
    Litigious men, which quarrels move,
    Though she and I do love.

Call us what you will, wee are made such by love;
    Call her one, mee another flye,
We'are Tapers too, and at out owne cost die,
      And wee in us finde the'Eagle and the Dove.
        The Phoenix riddle hath more wit
        By us, we two bing one, are it.
So to one neutrall thing both sexes fit,
    Wee die and rise the same, and prove
    Mysterious by this love.
Wee can die by it, if not live by love,
    And if unfit for tombes and hearse
Our legend bee, it will be fit for verse;

And if no peece of Chronicle wee prove,
   We'll build in sonnets pretty roomes;
   As well a well-wrought urne becomes
The greatest ashes, as half-acre tombes,
   And by these hymnes, all shall approve
   Us *Canoniz'd* for Love:

And thus invoke us; You whom reverend love
   Made one anothers hermitage;
You, to whom love was peace, that now is rage;
   Who did the whole worlds soule contract, and drove
     Into the glasses of your eyes
     (So made such mirrors, and such spies,
That they did all to you epitomize,)
   Countries, Townes, Courts: Beg from above
   A patterne of your love!

The Relique

When my grave is broke up againe
   Some second ghest to entertaine,
   (For graves have learn'd that woman-head
   To be to more than one a Bed)
   And he that digs it, spies
A bracelet of bright haire about the bone,
   Will he not let'us alone,
And thinke that there a loving couple lies,
Who thought that this device might be some way
To make thier soules, at the last busie day,
Meet at this grave, and make a little stay?
   If this fall in a time, or land,
   Where mis-devotion doth command,
   Then, he that digges us up, wil bring

Us, to the Bishop, and the King,
　　To make us Reliques; then
Thoug shalt be a Mary Magdalen, and I
　　A something else thereby;
All women shall adore us, and some men;
And since at such time, miracles are sought,
I would have that age by this paper taught
What miracles wee harmelesse lovers wroght.

First, we lov'd well and faithfully,
　　Yet knew not what wee lov'd, nor why,
Difference of sex no more wee knew,
　　Than our Guardian Angells doe;
　　　Coming and going, wee
Perchance might kisse, but not between those meales;
　　Our hands ne'er toucht the seales,
Which nature, injur'd by late law, sets free:
These miracles wee did; but now alas,
All measure, and all language, I should passe,
Should I tell what a miracle shee was.

Song

Go and catch a falling star,
　　Get with child a mandrake root,
Tell me where all past years are,
　　Or who cleft the Devil's foot;
Teach me to hear mermaids singing,
Or to keep off envy's stinging,
　　　And find
　　　What wind
Serves to advance an honest mind.

JOHN DONNE

If thou beest born to strange sights,
   Things invisible to see,
Ride ten thousand days and nights
   Till Age snow white hairs on thee;
Thou, when thou return'st, wilt tell me
All strange wonders that befell thee,
     And swear,
     No where
Lives a woman true and fair.

If thou find'st one, let me know;
   Such a pilgrimage were sweet.
Yet do not; I would not go,
   Though at next door we might meet.
Though she were true when you met her,
And last till you write your letter,
     Yet she
     Will be
False, ere I come, to two or three.

MICHAEL DRAYTON
1563-1631

Sonnet

iv

Since there's no help, come let us kiss and part.
 Nay, I have done; you get no more of me,
And I am glad, yea, glad with all my heart,
 That thus so cleanly I myself can free;
Shake hands for ever, cancel all our vows,
 And when we meet at any time again,
Be it not seen in either of our brows
 That we one jot of former love retain.
Now at the last gasp of Love's latest breath,
 When, his pulse failing, Passion speechless lies,
When Faith is kneeling by his bed of death,
 And Innocence is closing up his eyes,
  Now if thou wouldst, when all have given him over,
  From death to life thou mightst him yet recover.

To His Coy Love: A Canzonet

I pray thee leave, love me no more,
Call home the Heart you gave me,
 I but in vaine that Saint adore,
That can, but will not save me:

These poore halfe kisses kill me quite;
 Was ever man thus served?
Amidst an Ocean of Delight,
 For Pleasure to be sterved.

41

Shew me no more those Snowie Brests
    With Azure Riverets branched,
Where whilst mine Eye with Plentie feasts,
    Yet is my Thirst not stanched.
O Tantalus, thy Paines ne'er tell,
    By me thou are prevented;
'Tis nothing to be plagu'd in Hell,
    But thus in Heaven tormented.

Clip me no more in those deare Armes,
    Nor thy Life's Comfort call me;
O, these are but too pow'rfull Charmes,
    And doe but more inthrall me.
But see how patient I am growne,
    In all this coyle about thee;
Come nice Thing, let thy Heart alone,
    I cannot live without thee.

THOMAS FORD
d. 1648

There is a Lady sweet and kind

There is a Lady sweet and kind,
Was never face so pleas'd my mind;
I did but see her passing by,
And yet I love her till I die.

Her gesture, motion and her smiles,
Her wit, her voyce, my heart beguiles,
Beguiles my heart, I know not why,
And yet I love her till I die.

Her free behaviour, winning lookes,
Will make a Lawyer burne his bookes.
I touchd her not, alas, not I,
And yet I love her till I die.
Had I her fast betwixt mine armes,
Judge you that thinke such sports were harmes,
Wer't any harm? no, no, fie, fie!
For I will love her till I die.

Should I remaine confined there,
So long as Phebus in his sphere,
I to request, she to denie,
Yet would I love her till I die.

Cupid is winged and doth range,
Her countrie so my love doth change,
But change she earth, or change she skie,
Yet will I love her till I die.

GEORGE WITHER
1588-1667

A Lover's Resolution

Shall I, wasting in despair,
Die because a woman's fair?
Or make pale my cheeks with care
'Cause another's rosy are?
Be she fairer than the day,
Or the flowery meads in May,
   If she be not so to me,
   What care I how fair she be?

Should my heart be grieved or pined
'Cause I see a woman kind?
Or a well disposèd nature
Joinèd with a lovely feature?
Be she meeker, kinder, than
Turtle-dove or pelican,
   If she be not so to me,
   What care I how kind she be?

Shall a woman's virtues move
Me to perish for her love?
Or her well-deserving known
Make me quite forget mine own?
Be she with that goodness blest
Which may gain her name of Best,
   If she be not such to me,
   What care I how good she be?

'Cause her fortune seems too high,
Shall I play the fool and die?
Those that bear a noble mind,
Where they want of riches find,
Think what with them they would do
That without them dare to woo.
    And unless that mind I see,
    What care I though great she be?

Great, or good, or kind, or fair,
I will ne'er the more despair;
If she love me, this believe,
I will die ere she shall grieve.
If she slight me when I woo,
I can scorn and let her go.
    For if she be not for me,
    What care I for whom she be?

ROBERT HERRICK
1591-1674

Delight in Disorder

A sweet disorder in the dress
Kindles in clothes a wantonness:
A lawn about the shoulders thrown
Into a fine distraction:
An erring lace, which here and there
Enthrals the crimson stomacher:
A cuff neglectful, and thereby
Ribbands to flow confusedly:
A winning wave, deserving note,
In the tempestuous petticoat:
A careless shoe-string, in whose tie
I see a wild civility:
Do more bewitch me than when art
Is too precise in every part.

To Anthea, Who May Command Him Anything

Bid me to live, and I will live
　　Thy Protestant to be;
Or bid me love, and I will give
　　A loving heart to thee.

A heart as soft, a heart as kind,
　　A heart as sound and free
As in the whole world thou canst find,
　　That heart I'll give to thee.

ROBERT HERRICK

Bid that heart stay, and it will stay
   To honour thy decree:
Or bid it languish quite away,
   And 't shall do so for thee.

Bid me to weep, and I will weep
   While I have eyes to see:
And, having none, yet I will keep
   A heart to weep for thee.

Bid me despair, and I'll despair
   Under that cypress-tree:
Or bid me die, and I will dare
   E'en death to die for thee.

Thou art my life, my love, my heart,
   The very eyes of me:
And hast command of every part
   To live and die for thee.

To the Virgins, to Make Much of Time

Gather ye rosebuds while ye may,
   Old Time is still a-flying:
And this same flower that smiles to-day
   To-morrow will be dying.

The glorious lamp of heaven, the sun,
   The higher he's a-getting,
The sooner will his race be run,
   And nearer he's to setting.

That age is best which is the first,
    When youth and blood are warmer;
But being spent, the worse, and worst
    Times still succeed the former.

Then be not coy, but use your time,
    And while ye may, go marry:
For having lost but once your prime,
    You may for ever tarry.

To his Maid Prew

These *Summer-Birds* did with thy Master stay
The times of warmth; but then they flew away;
Leaving their Poet (being now grown old).

Expos'd to all the coming winters cold.
But thou *kind Prew* did'st with my Fates abide,
As well the Winters, as the Summers Tide:
For which thy Love, live with thy Master here,
Not two, but all the seasons of the yeare.

Upon Julia's Clothes

When as in silks my *Julia* goes,
Then, then (me thinks) how swettly flowes
That liquefaction of her clothes.

Next, when I cast mine eyes and see
That brave Vibration each way free;
O how that glittering taketh me!

The Night-piece to Julia

Her Eyes the Glow-worme lend thee,
  The Shooting Starres attend thee;
    And the Elves also,
    Whose little eyes glow,
Like the sparks of fire, befriend thee.

No *Will-o'-th'-Wispe* mis-light thee;
  Nor Snake, or Slow-worme bite thee:
    But on, on thy way
    Not making a stay,
Since Ghost there's none to affright thee.

Let not the darke thee cumber;
  What though the Moon does slumber?
    The Starres of the night
    Will lend thee their light,
Like Tapers cleare without number.

Then *Julia* let me wooe thee,
  Thus, thus to come unto me:
    And when I shall meet
    Thy silv'ry feet,
My soule I'll poure into thee.

EDMUND WALLER
1606-1687

On a Girdle

That which her slender waist confined
Shall now my joyful temples bind;
No monarch but would give his crown
His arms might do what this has done.

It was my Heaven's extremest sphere,
The pale which held that lovely deer:
My joy, my grief, my hope, my love,
Did all within this circle move.

A narrow compass! and yet there
Dwelt all that's good, and all that's fair!
Give me but what this ribband bound,
Take all the rest the sun goes round!

Go, Lovely Rose

Go, lovely Rose—
    Tell her that wastes her time and me,
    That now she knows,
When I resemble her to thee,
How sweet and fair she seems to be.

Tell her that's young,
And shuns to have her graces spied,
That hadst thou sprung
In deserts where no men abide,
Thou must have uncommended died.

Small is the worth
Of beauty from the light retired:
Bid her come forth,
Suffer herself to be desired,
And not blush so to be admired.

Then die—that she
The common fate of all things rare
May read in thee;
How small a part of time they share
That are so wondrous sweet and fair!

ANDREW MARVELL
1621-1678

To His Coy Mistress

Had we but world enough, and time,
This coyness, Lady, were no crime.
We would sit down and think which way
To walk and pass our long love's day.
Thou by the Indian Ganges' side
Shouldst rubies find: I by the tide
Of Humber would complain. I would
Love you ten years before the Flood,
And you should, if you please, refuse
Till the conversion of the Jews.
My vegetable love should grow
Vaster than empires, and more slow;
An hundred years should go to praise
Thine eyes and on thy forehead gaze;
Two hundred to adore each breast;
But thirty thousand to the rest;
An age at least to every part,
And the last age should show your heart;
For, Lady, you deserve this state,
Nor would I love at lower rate.
    But at my back I always hear
Time's winged chariot hurrying near;
And yonder all before us lie
Deserts of vast eternity.
Thy beauty shall no more be found,
Nor, in thy marble vault, shall sound
My echoing song: then worms shall try

ANDREW MARVELL

That long preserved virginity,
And your quaint honour turn to dust,
And into ashes all my lust:
The grave's a fine and private place,
But none, I think, do there embrace.
    Now therefore, while the youthful hue
Sits on thy skin like morning dew,
And while thy willing soul transpires
At every pore with instant fires,
Now let us sport us while we may,
And now, like amorous birds of prey,
Rather at once our time devour
Than languish in his slow-chapt power.
Let us roll all our strength and all
Our sweetness up into one ball,
And tear our pleasures with rough strife
Thorough the iron gates of life:
Thus, though we cannot make our sun
Stand still, yet we will make him run.

THOMAS STANLEY
1625-1678

The Magnet

Ask the Empress of the night
　How the hand which guides her sphere,
Constant in unconstant light,
　Taught the waves her yoke to bear,
And did thus by loving force
Curb or tame the rude sea's course.

Ask the female palm how she
　First did woo her husband's love;
And the magnet, ask how he
　Doth the obsequious iron move;
Waters, plants and stones know this,
That they love, not what love is.

Be not then less kind than these,
　Or from love exempt alone;
Let us twine like amorous trees,
　And like rivers melt in one;
Or if thou more cruel prove
Learn of steel and stones to love.

JOHN WILMOT, EARL OF ROCHESTER
1647-1680

The Mistress

An age in her embraces passed
  Would seem a winter's day,
Where life and light with envious haste
  Are torn and snatched away.

But oh, how slowly minutes roll
  When absent from her eyes,
That feed my love, which is my soul:
  It languishes and dies.

For then no more a soul, but shade,
  It mournfully does move
And haunts my breast, by absence made
  The living tomb of love.

You wiser men, despise me not
  Whose lovesick fancy raves
On shades of souls, and heaven knows what:
  Short age live in graves.

Whene'er those wounding eyes, so full
  Of sweetness, you did see,
Had you not been profoundly dull,
  You had gone mad like me.

JOHN WILMOT, EARL OF ROCHESTER

Nor censure us, you who perceive
    My best beloved and me
Sigh and lament, complain and grieve:
    You think we disagree.

Alas! 'tis sacred jealousy,
    Love raised to an extreme:
The only proof 'twixt her and me
    We love, and do not dream.

Fantastic fancies fondly move
    And in frail joys believe,
Taking false pleasure for true love;
    But pain can ne'er deceive.

Kind jealous doubts, tormenting fears,
    And anxious cares, when past,
Prove our hearts' treasure fixed and dear,
    And make us blest at last.

APHRA BEHN
1640-1689

Song

Love in fantastic triumph sate
   Whilst bleeding hearts around him flowed,
For whom fresh pains he did create
   And strange tyrannic power he showed:
From thy bright eyes he took his fires,
   Which round about in sport he hurled;
But 'twas from mine he took desires
   Enough to undo the amorous world.

From me he took his sighs and tears,
   From thee his pride and cruelty';
From me his languishments and fears,
   And every killing dart from thee.
Thus thou and I the god have armed
   And set him up a deity;
But my poor heart alone is harmed,
   Whilst thine the victor is, and free!

JOHN DRYDEN
1631-1700

Farewell, Ungrateful Traitor

Farewell, ungrateful traitor,
Farewell, my perjured swain,
Let never injured creature
Believe a man again.
The pleasure of possessing
Surpasses all expressing,
But 'tis too short a blessing,
And love too long a pain.

'Tis easy to deceive us
In pity of your pain,
But when we love you leave us
To rail at you in vain.
Before we have descried it
There is no bliss beside it,
But she that once has tried it
Will never love again.

JOHN DRYDEN

The passion you pretended
Was only to obtain,
But when the charm is ended
The charmer you disdain.
Your love by ours we measure
Till we have lost our treasure,
But dying is a pleasure,
When living is a pain.

SIR CHARLES SEDLEY
1639-1701

Song

Love still has something of the sea,
  From whence his mother rose;
No time his slaves from Doubt can free,
  Nor give their thoughts repose:

They are becalmed in clearest days,
  And in rough weather tost;
They wither under cold delays,
  Or are in tempests lost.

One while they seem to touch the port,
  Then straight into the main,
Some angry wind in cruel sport
  The vessel drives again.

At first Disdain and Pride they fear,
  Which if they chance to 'scape,
Rivals and Falsehood soon appear
  In a more dreadful shape.

By such degrees to Joy they come,
  And are so long withstood,
So slowly they receive the sum,
  It hardly does them good.

'Tis cruel to prolong a pain,
　　And to defer a joy,
Believe me, gentle Celemene,
　　Offends the winged Boy.

An hundred thousand oaths your fears
　　Perhaps would not remove;
And if I gazed a thousand years
　　I could no deeper love.

Phyllis Knotting

Hears not my Phyllis how the birds
　　Their feathered mates salute?
They tell their passion in their words;
　　Must I alone be mute?
Phyllis, *without frown or smile,*
Sat and knotted all the while.

The God of Love in thy bright eyes
　　Does like a tyrant reign;
But in thy heart a child he lies,
　　Without his dart or flame.
Phyllis, *without frown or smile,*
Sat and knotted all the while.

So many months in silence past,
    And yet in raging love,
Might well deserve one word at last
    My passion should approve.
Phyllis, *without frown or smile,*
Sat and knotted all the while.

Must then your faithful swain expire,
    And not one look obtain,
Which he, to sooth his fond desire,
    Might pleasingly explain?
Phyllis, *without frown or smile,*
Sat and knotted all the while.

MATTHEW PRIOR
1664-1721

Answer to Chloe Jealous

Dear Chloe, how blubbered is that pretty face!
Thy cheek all on fire, and thy hair all uncurled.
Prithee, quit this caprice; and (as old Falstaff says)
Let us e'en talk a little like folks of this world.

How canst thou presume thou hast leave to destroy
The beauties which Venus but lent to thy keeping?
Those looks were designed to inspire love and joy:
More ordinary eyes may serve people for weeping.

To be vexed at a trifle or two that I writ
Your judgement at once and my passion you wrong:
You take that for fact which will scarce be found wit:
'Od's life! must one swear to the truth of a song?

What I speak, my fair Chloe, and what I write, shows
The difference there is betwixt Nature and Aart:
I court others in verse, but I love thee in prose;
And they have my whimsies, but thou hast my heart.

The God of us verse-men, you know, child, the sun
How after his journeys he sets up his rest:
If at morning o'er Earth 'tis his fancy to run,
At night he reclines on his Thetis's breast.

So when I am wearied with wandering all day,
To thee, my delight, in the evening I come;
No matter what beauties I saw in my way,
They were but my visits, but thou art my home.

Then finish, dear Chloe, this pastoral war,
And let us like Horace and Lydia agree:
For thou art a girl as much brighter than her
As he was a poet sublimer than me.

ALEXANDER POPE
1688-1744

Chloe

'Yet Chloe sure was formed without a spot'—
Nature in her then erred not, but forgot.
'With every pleasing, every prudent part,
Say, what can Chloe want?'—She wants a heart.
She speaks, behaves, and acts just as she ought;
But never, never, reached one generous thought.
Virtue she finds too painful an endeavour,
Content to dwell in decencies forever.
So very reasonable, so unmoved,
As never yet to love, or to be loved.
She, while her lover pants upon her breast,
Can mark the figures on an Indian chest;
And when she sees her friend in deep despair,
Observes how much a chintz exceeds mohair.
Forbid it Heaven, a favour or a debt
She e'er should cancel—but she may forget.
Safe is your secret still in Chloe's ear;
But none of Chloe's shall you ever hear.
Of all her Dears she never slandered one,
But cares not if a thousand are undone.
Would Chloe know if you're alive or dead?
She bids her foootman put it in her head.
Chloe is prudent—would you too be wise?
Then never break your heart when Chloe dies.

LADY MARY WORTLEY MANTAGU
1689-1762

A Receipt to Cure the Vapours

Why will Delia thus retire,
　　And idly languish life away?
While the sighing crowd admire,
　　'Tis too soon for hartshorn tea.

All those dismal looks and fretting
　　Cannot Damon's life restore;
Long ago the worms have ate him,
　　You can never see him more.

Once again consult your toilette,
　　In the glass your face review:
So much weeping soon will spoil it,
　　And no spring your charms renew.

I, like you, was born a woman,
　　Well I know what vapours mean:
The disease, alas! is common;
　　Single, we have all the spleen.

All the morals that they tell us
　　Never cured the sorrow yet:
Choose, among the pretty fellows,
　　One of honour, youth and wit.

Prithee hear him every morning,
　　At the least an hour or two;
Once again at night returning—
　　I believe the dose will do.

FRANNY GREVILLE
18th Century

Prayer for Indifference

I ask no kind return of love,
   No tempting charm to please;
Far from the heart those gifts remove,
   That sighs for peace and ease.

Nor peace nor ease the heart can know,
   That, like the needle true,
Turns at the touch of joy or woe,
   But, turning, trembles too.

Far as distress the soul can wound,
   'Tis pain in each degree:
'Tis bliss but to a certain bound,
   Beyond is agong.

WALTER SAVAGE LANDOR
1775-1864

Rose Aylmer

Ah, what avails the sceptred race!
  Ah, what the form divine!
What every virtue, every grace!
  Rose Aylmer, all were thine.

Rose Aylmer, whom these wakeful eyes
  May weep, but never see,
A night of memories and sighs
  I consecrate to thee.

I strove with none

I strove with none, for none was worth my strife.
Nature I loved and, next to Nature, Art:
I warmed both hands before the fire of life;
  It sinks, and I am ready to depart.

JOHN KEATS
1795-1821

La Belle Dame Sans Merci

'O what can ail thee, knight-at-arms,
    Alone and palely loitering?
The sedge has withered from the lake,
    And no birds sing.

'O what can ail thee, knight-at-arms,
    So haggard and so woe-begone?
The squirrel's granary is full,
    And the harvest's done.

'I see a lily on thy brow
    With anguish moist and fever dew;
And on thy cheek a fading rose
    Fast withereth too.'

'I met a lady in the meads,
    Full beautiful—a faery's child,
Her hair was long, her foot was light,
    And her eyes were wild.

'I made a garland for her head,
    And bracelets too, and fragrant zone;
She looked at me as she did love,
    And made sweet moan.

JOHN KEATS

'I set her on my pacing steed
    And nothing else saw all day long,
For sideways would she lean, and sing
    A faery's song.

'She found me roots of relish sweet,
    And honey wild and manna dew,
And sure in language strange she said,
    "I love thee true!"

'She took me to her elfin grot,
    And there she wept and sighed full sore;
And there I shut her wild, wild eyes
    With kisses four.

'And there she lulled me asleep,
    And there I dreamed—Ah! woe betide!
The latest dream I ever dreamed
    On the cold hill's side.

'I saw pale kings and princes too,
    Pale warriors, death-pale were they all;
Who cried—"La belle Dame sans Merci
    Hath thee in thrall!"

'I saw their starved lips in the gloam
    With horrid warning gaped wide,
And I awoke and found me here
    On the cold hill's side.

'And this is why I sojourn here
    Alone and palely loitering,
Though the sedge is withered from the lake,
    And no birds sing.'

Last Sonnet

Bright star, would I were steadfast as thou art—
   Not in lone splendour hung aloft the night,
And watching, with eternal lids apart,
   Like Nature's patient sleepless Eremite,
The moving waters at their priest-like task
   Of pure ablution round earth's human shores,
Or gazing on the new soft-fallen mask
   Of snow upon the mountains and the moors—
No—yet still steadfast, still unchangeable,
   Pillowed upon my fair love's ripening breast,
To feel for ever its soft fall and swell,
   Awake for ever in a sweet unrest,
     Still, still to hear her tender-taken breath,
     And so live ever—or else swoon to death.

To Fanny Brawne

This living hand, now warm and capable
Of earnest grasping, would, if it were cold
And in the icy silence of the tomb,
So haunt thy days and chill thy dreaming nights
That thou wouldst wish thine own heart dry of blood
So in my veins red life might stream again,
And thou be conscience-calmed—see here it is—
I hold it towards you.

THOMAS HOOD
1799-1845

Ruth

She stood breast high amid the corn,
Clasped by the golden light of morn,
Like the sweetheart of the sun,
Who many a glowing kiss had won.

On her cheek an autumn flush,
Deeply ripened;—such a blush
In the midst of brown was born,
Like red poppies grown with corn.

Round her eyes her tresses fell,
Which were blackest none could tell,
But long lashes veiled a light,
That had else been all too bright.

And her hat, with shady brim,
Made her tressy forehead dim;—
Thus she stood amid the stooks,
Praising God with sweetest looks:—

Sure, I said, heaven did not mean,
Where I reap thou shouldst but glean,
Lay thy sheaf adown and come,
Share my harvest and my home.

PERCY BYSSHE SHELLEY
1792-1822

Lines

When the lamp is shatter'd
The light in the dust lies dead;
When the cloud is scatter'd,
The rainbow's glory is shed;
When the lute is broken,
Sweet tones are remember'd not;
When the lips have spoken,
Loved accents are soon forgot.

As music and splendour
Survive not the lamp and the lute,
The heart's echoes render
No song when the spirit is mute—
No song but sad dirges,
Like the wind through a ruin'd cell,
Or the mournful surges
That ring the dead seaman's knell.

When hearts have once mingled,
Love first leaves the well-built nest;
The weak one is singled
To endure what it once possest.
O Love, who bewailest
The frailty of all things here,
Why choose you the frailest
For your cradle, your home, and your bier?

Its passions will rock thee,
As the storms rock the ravens on high:
   Bright reason will mock thee,
Like the sun from a wintry sky.
   From thy nest every rafter
Will rot, and thine eagle home
   Leave thee naked to laughter,
When leaves fall and cold winds come.

To—

One word is too often profaned
   For me to profane it;
One feeling too falsely disdain'd
   For thee to disdain it;
One hope is too like despair
   For prudence to smother;
And pity from thee more dear
   Than that from another.

I can give not what men call love:
   But wilt thou accept not
The worship the heart lifts above
   And the heavens reject not,
The desire of the moth for the star,
   Of the night for the morrow,
The devotion to something afar
   From the sphere of our sorrow?

Song

A widow bird sate mourning for her love
    Upon a wintry bough;
The frozen wind crept on above,
    The freezing stream below.

There was no leaf upon the forest bare,
    No flower upon the ground,
And little motion in the air
    Except the mill-wheel's sound.

GEORGE GORDON NOEL, LORD BYRON
1788-1824

She walks in beauty, like the night

Of cloudless climes and starry skies;
And all that's best of dark and bright
   Meet in her aspect and her eyes:
Thus mellowed to that tender light
   Which heaven to gaudy day denies.

One shade the more, one ray the less,
   Had half impaired the nameless grace
Which waves in every raven tress,
   Or softly lightens o'er her face;
Where thoughts serenely sweet express
   How pure, how dear their dwelling-place.

And on that cheek, and o'er that brow,
   So soft, so calm, yet eloquent,
The smiles that win, the tints that glow,
   But tell of days in gooodness spent,
A mind at peace with all below,
   A heart whose love is innocent.

So, we'll go no more a-roving

So, we'll go no more a-roving
   So late into the night,
Though the heart be still as loving,
   And the moon be still as bright.

For the sword outwears its sheath,
  And the soul wears out the breast,
And the heart must pause to breathe,
  And love itself have rest.

Though the night was made for loving,
  And the day returns too soon,
Yet we'll go no more a-roving
  By the light of the moon.

When we two parted

When we two parted
  In silence and tears,
Half broken-hearted
  To sever for years,
Pale grew thy cheek and cold,
  Colder thy kiss;
Truly that hour foretold
  Sorrow to this.

The dew of the morning
  Sunk chill on my brow—
It felt like the warning
  Of what I feel now.
Thy vows are all broken,
  And light is thy fame;
I hear thy name spoken,
  And share in its shame.

They name thee before me,
    A knell to mine ear;
A shudder comes o'er me—
    Why wert thou so dear?
They know not I knew thee,
    Who knew thee too well:—
Long, long shall I rue thee,
    Too deeply to tell.

In secret we met—
    In silence I grieve,
That thy heart could forget,
    Thy spirit deceive.
If I should meet thee
    After long years,
How should I greet thee?
    With silence and tears.

WILLIAM BLAKE
1757-1827

Never Seek to Tell Thy Love

Never seek to tell thy love
Love that never told can be;
For the gentle wind does move
Silently, invisibly.

I told my love, I told my love,
I told her all my heart,
Trembling, cold, in ghastly fears—
Ah, she doth depart.

Soon as she was gone from me
A traveller came by
Silently, invisibly—
O, was no deny.

The Prince of Love

How sweet I roamed from field to field,
    And tasted all the summer's pride,
'Till I the prince of love beheld,
    Who in the sunny beams did glide!

He showed me lilies for my hair,
    And blushing roses for my brow;
He led me through his gardens fair,
    Where all his golden pleasures grow.

With sweet May dews my wings were wet,
   And Phoebus fired my vocal rage;
He caught me in his silken net,
   And shut me in his golden cage.

He loves to sit and hear me sing,
   Then, laughing, sports and plays with me;
Then stretches out my golden wing,
   And mocks my loss of liberty.

The Divine Image

To Mercy, Pity, Peace, and Love
All pray in their distress;
And to these virtues of delight
Return their thankfulness.

For Mercy, Pity, Peace, and Love
Is God, our father dear,
And Mercy, Pity, Peace, and Love,
Is Man, his child and care.

For Mercy has a human heart,
Pity a human face,
And Love, the human form divine,
And Peace, the human dress.

Then every man, of every clime,
That prays in his distress,
Prays to the human form divine,
Love, Mercy, Pity, Peace.

And all must love the human form,
In heathen, turk, or jew;
Where Mercy, Love, and Pity dwell
There God is dwelling too.

The Clod and the Pebble

'Love seeketh not itself to please,
Nor for itself hath any care,
But for another gives it ease,
And builds a Heaven in Hell's despair.'

So sung a little Clod of Clay
Trodden with the cattle's feet,
But a Pebble of the brook
Warbled out these metres meet:

'Love seeketh only self to please,
To bind another to its delight,
Joys in another's loss of ease,
And builds a Hell in Heaven's despite.'

GEORGE CRABBE
1754-1832

Meeting

My Damon was the first to wake
  The gentle flame that cannot die;
My Damon is the last to take
  The faithful bosom's softest sigh:
The life between is nothing worth,
  O cast it from thy thought away!
Think of the day that gave it birth,
  And this its sweet returning day.

Buried be all that has been done,
  Or say that naught is done amiss;
For who the dangerous path can shun
  In such bewildering world as this?
But love can every fault forgive,
  Or with a tender look reprove;
And now let naught in memory live
  But that we meet, and that we love.

His Late Wife's Wedding-Ring

The ring so worn, as you behold,
So thin, so pale, is yet of gold:
The passion such it was to prove;
Worn with life's cares, love yet was love.

WILLIAM WORDSWORTH
1770-1850

Lucy

(i)

Strange fits of passion have I known:
And I will dare to tell,
But in the Lover's ear alone,
What once to me befell.

When she I loved looked every day
Fresh as a rose in June,
I to her cottage bent my way,
Beneath an evening-moon.

Upon the moon I fixed my eye,
All over the wide lea;
With quickening pace my horse drew nigh
Those paths so dear to me.

And now we reached the orchard-plot;
And, as we climbed the hill,
The sinking moon to Lucy's cot
Came near, and nearer still.

In one of those sweet dreams I slept,
Kind Nature's gentlest boon!
And all the while my eyes I kept
On the descending moon.

My horse moved on; hoof after hoof
He raised, and never stopped:
When down behind the cottage roof,
At once, the bright moon dropped.

What fond and wayward thoughts will slide
Into a Lover's head!
'O mercy!' to myself I cried,
'If Lucy should be dead!'

(ii)

She dwelt among the untrodden ways
Beside the springs of Dove,
A Maid whom there were none to praise
And very few to love:

A violet by a mossy stone
Half hidden from the eye!
Fair as a star, when only one
Is shining in the sky.

She lived unknown, and few could know
When Lucy ceased to be;
But she is in her grave, and oh,
The difference to me!

A Complaint

There is a change—and I am poor;
Your love hath been, nor long ago,
A fountain at my fond heart's door,
Whose only business was to flow;
And flow it did; not taking heed
Of its own bounty, or my need.

What happy moments did I count!
Blest was I then all bliss above!
Now, for that consecrated fount
Of murmuring, sparkling, living love,
What have I? shall I dare to tell?
A comfortless and hidden well.

A well of love—it may be deep—
I trust it is,—and never dry:
What matter? if the waters sleep
In silence and obscurity.
—Such change, and at the very door
Of my fond heart, hath made me poor.

Surprised by joy

Surprised by joy—impatient as the wind
I turned to share the transport—Oh! with whom
But thee, deep buried in the silent tomb,
That spot which no vicissitude can find?

Love, faithful love, recalled thee to my mind—
  But how could I forget thee? Through what power,
  Even for the least division of an hour,
Have I been so beguiled as to be blind
To my most grievous loss!—That thought's return
  Was the worst pang that sorrow ever bore,
Save one, one only, when I stood forlorn,
  Knowing my heart's best treasure was no more;
That neither present time, nor years unborn
  Could to my sight that heavenly face restore.

JAMES LEIGH HUNT
1784-1859

Jenny Kissed Me

Jenny kissed me when we met,
  Jumping from the chair she sat in;
Time, you thief, who love to get
  Sweets into your list, put that in!
Say I'm weary, say I'm sad,
  Say that health and wealth have missed me,
Say I'm growing old, but add,
  Jenny kissed me.

JOHN CLARE
1793-1864

Love lives beyond

Love lives beyond
The tomb, the earth, which fades like dew!
    I love the fond,
The faithful, and the true.

Love lives in sleep,
The happiness of healthy dreams:
    Eve's dews may weep,
But love delightful seems.

'Tis seen in flowers,
And in the morning's pearly dew;
    In earth's green hours,
And in the heaven's eternal blue.

'Tis heard in spring
When light and sunbeams, warm and kind,
    On angel's wing
Bring love and music to the mind.

And where is voice,
So young, so beautiful, and sweet
    As nature's choice,
Where spring and lovers meet?

Love lives beyond
The tomb, the earth, the flowers, and dew.
    I love the fond,
The faithful, young, and true.

ELIZABETH BARRETT BROWNING
1806-1861

Sonnets from the Portuguese

(i)

I thought once how Theocritus had sung
   Of the sweet years, the dear and wished-for years,
   Who each one in a gracious hand appears
To bear a gift for mortals, old or young:
And, as I mused it in his antique tongue,
   I saw, in gradual vision through my tears,
   The sweet, sad years, the melancholy years,
Those of my own life, who by turns had flung
A shadow across me. Straightway I was 'ware,
   So weeping, how a mystic Shape did move
Behind me, and drew me backward by the hair;
   And a voice said in mastery, while I strove,—
'Guess now who holds thee?'—'Death,' I said. But, there,
   The silver answer rang,—'Not Death, but Love.'

(ii)

If thou must love me, let it be for naught
   Except for love's sake only. Do not say,
   'I love her for her smile—her look—her way
Of speaking gently,—for a trick of thought
That falls in well with mine, and certes brought
   A sense of pleasant ease on such a day'—
   For these things in themselves, Beloved, may
Be changed, or change for thee—and love, so wrought,
May be unwrought so. Neither love me for

Thine own dear pity's wiping my cheeks dry:
A creature might forget to weep, who bore
   Thy comfort long, and lose thy love thereby!
But love me for love's sake, that evermore
   Thou mayst love on, through love's eternity.

(iii)

When our two souls stand up erect and strong,
   Face to face, silent, drawing nigh and nigher,
   Until the lengthening wings break into fire
At either curved point,—what bitter wrong
Can the earth do to us, that we should not long
   Be here contented? Think! In mounting higher,
   The angels would press on us, and aspire
To drop some golden orb of perfect song
Into our deep, dear silence. Let us stay
   Rather on earth, Beloved—where the unfit
Contrarious moods of men recoil away
   And isolate pure spirits, and permit
A place to stand and love in for a day,
   With darkness and the death-hour rounding it.

ROBERT BROWNING
1812-1889

Meeting at Night

The gray sea and the long black land;
And the yellow half-moon large and low;
And the startled little waves that leap
In fiery ringlets from their sleep,
As I gain the cove with pushing prow,
And quench its speed i' the slushy sand.

Then a mile of warm sea-scented beach;
Three fields to cross till a farm appears;
A tap at the pane, the quick sharp scratch
And blue spurt of a lighted match,
And a voice less loud, through its joys and fears,
Than the two hearts beating each to each!

Love in a Life

Room after room,
I hunt the house through
We inhabit together.
Heart, fear nothing, for, heart, thou shalt find her—
Next time, herself!—not the trouble behind her
Left in the curtain, the couch's perfume!
As she brushed it, the cornice-wreath blossomed anew:
Yon looking-glass gleamed at the wave of her feather.

Yet the day wears,
And door succeeds door;

I try the fresh fortune—
Range the wide house from the wing to the centre.
Still the same chance! she goes out as I enter.
Spend my whole day in the quest,—who cares?
But 'tis twilight, you see,—with such suites to explore,
Such closets to search, such alcoves to importune!

Two in the Campagna

I wonder do you feel to-day
    As I have felt since, hand in hand,
We sat down on the grass, to stray
    In spirit better through the land,
This morn of Rome and May?

For me, I touched a thought, I know,
    Has tantalized me many times,
(Like turns of thread the spiders throw
    Mocking across our path) for rhymes
To catch at and let go.

Help me to hold it! First it left
    The yellowing fennel, run to seed
There, branching from the brickwork's cleft,
    Some old tomb's ruin: yonder weed
Took up the floating weft,

Where one small orange cup amassed
    Five beetles,—blind and green they grope
Among the honey-meal: and last,
    Everywhere on the grassy slope
I traced it. Hold it fast!

The champaign with its endless fleece
    Of feathery grasses everywhere!
Silence and passion, joy and peace,
    An everlasting wash of air—
Rome's ghost since her decease.

Such life here, through such lengths of hours,
    Such miracles performed in play,
Such primal naked forms of flowers,
    Such letting nature have her way
While heaven looks from its towers!

How say you? Let us, O my dove,
    Let us be unashamed of soul,
As earth lies bare to heaven above!
    How is it under our control
To love or not to love?

I would that you were all to me,
    You that are just so much, no more.
Nor yours nor mine, nor slave nor free!
    Where does the fault lie? What the core
O' the wound, since wound must be?

I would I could adopt your will,
    See with your eyes, and set my heart
Beating by yours, and drink my fill
    At your soul's springs,—your part my part
In life, for good and ill.

No. I yearn upward, touch you close,
    Then stand away. I kiss your cheek,
Catch your soul's warmth,—I pluck the rose
    And love it more than tongue can speak—
Then the good minute goes.

Already how am I so far
    Out of that minute? Must I go
Still like the thistle-ball, no bar,
    Onward, whenever light winds blow,
Fixed by no friendly star?

Just when I seemed about to learn!
    Where is the thread now? Off again!
The old trick! Only I discern—
    Infinite passion, and the pain
Of finite hearts that yearn.

ALFRED, LORD TENNYSON
1809-1892

Now Sleeps the Crimson Petal

Now sleeps the crimson petal, now the white;
Nor waves the cypress in the palace walk;
Nor winks the gold fin in the porphyry font:
The fire-fly wakens: waken thou with me.

Now droops the milkwhite peacock like a ghost,
And like a ghost she glimmers on to me.

Now lies the Earth all Danaë to the stars,
And all thy heart lies open unto me.

Now slides the silent meteor on, and leaves
A shining furrow, as thy thoughts in me.

Now folds the lily all her sweetness up,
And slips into the bosom of the lake:
So fold thyself, my dearest, thou, and slip
Into my bosom and be lost in me.

Come into the garden, Maud

Come into the garden, Maud,
   For the black bat, night, has flown,
Come into the garden, Maud,
   I am here at the gate alone;
And the woodbine spices are wafted abroad,
   And the musk of the rose is blown.

For a breeze of morning moves,
   And the planet of Love is on high,
Beginning to faint in the light that she loves
   On a bed of daffodil sky,
To faint in the light of the sun she loves,
   To faint in his light, and to die.

All night have the roses heard
   The flute, violin, bassoon;
All night has the casement jasmine stirred
   To the dancers dancing in tune;
Till a silence fell with the waking bird,
   And a hush with the setting moon.

I said to the lily, 'There is but one
   With whom she has heart to be gay.
When will the dancers leave her alone?
   She is weary of dance and play.'
Now half to the setting moon are gone,
   And half to the rising day;
Low on the sand and loud on the stone
   The last wheel echoes away.

I said to the rose, 'The brief night goes
   In babble and revel and wine.
O young lord-lover, what sighs are those,
   For one that will never be thine?
But mine, but mine,' so I sware to the rose,
   'For ever and ever, mine.'

And the soul of the rose went into my blood,
    As the music clashed in the hall;
And long by the garden lake I stood,
    For I heard your rivulet fall
From the lake to the meadow and on to the wood,
    Our wood, that is dearer than all;

From the meadow your walks have left so sweet
    That whenever a March-wind sighs
He sets the jewel-print of your feet
    In violets blue as your eyes,
To the woody hollows in which we meet
    And the valleys of Paradise.

The slender acacia would not shake
    One long milk-bloom on the tree;
The white lake-blossom fell into the lake
    As the pimpernel dozed on the lea;
But the rose was awake all night for your sake,
    Knowing your promise to me;
The lilies and roses were all awake,
    They sighed for the dawn and thee.

Queen rose of the rosebud garden of girls,
    Come hither, the dances are done,
In gloss of satin and glimmer of pearls,
    Queen lily and rose in one;
Shine out, little head, sunning over with curls,
    To the flowers, and be their sun.

There has fallen a splendid tear
   From the passion-flower at the gate.
She is coming, my dove, my dear;
   She is coming, my life, my fate;
The red rose cries, 'She is near, she is near;'
   And the white rose weeps, 'She is late;'
The larkspur listens, 'I hear, I hear;'
   And the lily whispers, 'I wait.'

She is coming, my own, my sweet,
   Were it ever so airy a tread,
My heart would hear her and beat,
   Were it earth in an earthy bed;
My dust would hear her and beat,
   Had I lain for a century dead;
Would start and tremble under her feet,
   And blossom in purple and red.

In the Valley of Cauteretz

All along the valley, stream that flashest white,
Deepening thy voice with the deepening of the night,
All along the valley, where thy waters flow,
I walked with one I loved two and thirty years ago.
All along the valley, while I walked today,
The two and thirty years were a mist that rolls away;
For all along the valley, down thy rocky bed,
Thy living voice to me was as the voice of the dead,
And all along the valley, by rock and cave and tree,
The voice of the dead was a living voice to me.

EMILY BRONTË
1818-1848

The Visionary

Silent is the house: all are laid asleep:
One alone looks out o'er the snow-wreaths deep,
Watching every cloud, dreading every breeze
That whirls the wildering drift, and bends the groaning trees.

Cheerful is the hearth, soft the matted floor;
Not one shivering gust creeps through pane or door;
The little lamp burns straight, its rays shoot strong and far:
I trim it well, to be the wanderer's guiding-star.

Frown, my haughty sire! chide, my angry dame;
Set your slaves to spy; threaten me with shame:
But neither sire nor dame, nor prying serf shall know,
What angel nightly tracks that waste of frozen snow.

What I love shall come like visitant of air,
Safe in secret power from lurking human snare;
Who loves me, no word of mine shall e'er betray,
Though for faith unstained my life must forfeit pay.

Burn, then, little lamp; glimmer straight and clear—
Hush! a rustling wing stirs, methinks, the air:
He for whom I wait, thus ever comes to me;
Strange Power! I trust thy might; trust thou my constancy.

MATTHEW ARNOLD
1822-1888

Dover Beach

The sea is calm to-night.
The tide is full, the moon lies fair
Upon the straits;—on the French coast the light
Gleams and is gone; the cliffs of England stand,
Glimmering and vast, out in the tranquil bay.
Come to the window, sweet is the night-air!
Only, from the long line of spray
Where the sea meets the moon-blanched land,
Listen! you hear the grating roar
Of pebbles which the waves draw back, and fling,
At their return, up the high strand,
Begin, and cease, and then again begin,
With tremulous cadence slow, and bring
The eternal note of sadness in.

Sophocles long ago
Heard it on the Ægæan, and it brought
Into his mind the turbid ebb and flow
Of human misery; we
Find also in the sound a thought,
Hearing it by this distant northern sea.

The Sea of Faith
Was once, too, at the full, and round earth's shore
Lay like the folds of a bright girdle furled.
But now I only hear
Its melancholy, long, withdrawing roar,
Retreating, to the breath
Of the night-wind, down the vast edges drear
And naked shingles of the world.

Ah, love, let us be true
To one another! for the world, which seems
To lie before us like a land of dreams,
So various, so beautiful, so new,
Hath really neither joy, nor love, nor light,
Nor certitude, nor peace, nor help for pain;
And we are here as on a darkling plain
Swept with confused alarms of struggle and flight,
Where ignorant armies clash by night.

CHRISTINA GEORGINA ROSSETTI
1830-1894

A Birthday

My heart is like a singing bird
    Whose nest is in a watered shoot;
My heart is like an apple-tree
    Whose boughs are bent with thickset fruit;
My heart is like a rainbow shell
    That paddles in a halcyon sea;
My heart is gladder than all these
    Because my love is come to me.

Raise me a dais of silk and down;
    Hang it with vair and purple dyes;
Carve it in doves and pomegranates,
    And peacocks with a hundred eyes;
Work it in gold and silver grapes,
    In leaves and silver fleurs-de-lys;
Because the birthday of my life
    Is come, my love is come to me.

Song

When I am dead, my dearest,
    Sing no sad songs for me;
Plant thou no roses at my head,
    Nor shady cypress tree:

Be the green grass above me
    With showers and dewdrops wet;
And if thou wilt, remember,
    And if thou wilt, forget.

I shall not see the shadows,
    I shall not feel the rain;
I shall not hear the nightingale
    Sing on, as if in pain;
And dreaming through the twilight
    That doth not rise nor set,
Haply I may remember,
    And haply may forget.

Remember

Remember me when I am gone away,
    Gone far away into the silent land;
    When you can no more hold me by the hand,
Nor I half turn to go yet turning stay.
Remember me when no more day by day
    You tell me of our future that you planned:
    Only remember me; you understand
It will be late to counsel then or pray.
Yet if you should forget me for a while
    And afterwards remember, do not grieve:
    For if the darkness and corruption leave
    A vestige of the thoughts that once I had,
Better by far you should forget and smile
    Than that you should remember and be sad.

Echo

Come to me in the silence of the night;
   Come in the speaking silence of a dream;
Come with soft rounded cheeks and eyes as bright
   As sunlight on a stream;
     Come back in tears,
O memory, hope, love of finished years.

O dream how sweet, too sweet, too bitter sweet,
   Whose wakening should have been in Paradise,
Where souls brimfull of love abide and meet;
   Where thirsting longing eyes
     Watch the slow door
That opening, letting in, lets out no more.

Yet come to me in dreams that I may live
   My very life again though cold in death:
Come back to me in dreams, that I may give
   Pulse for pulse, breath for breath:
     Speak low, lean low,
As long ago, my love, how long ago.

Twice

I took my heart in my hand
   (O my love, O my love),
I said: Let me fall or stand,
   Let me live or die,
But this once hear me speak—
   (O my love, O my love)—
Yet a woman's words are weak;
   You should speak, not I.

You took my heart in your hand
    With a friendly smile,
With a critical eye you scanned,
    Then set it down,
And said: It is still unripe,
    Better wait awhile;
Wait while the skylarks pipe,
    Till the corn grows brown.

As yet set it down it broke—
    Broke, but I did not wince;
I smiled at the speech you spoke,
    At your judgement that I heard:
But I have not often smiled
    Since then, nor questioned since,
Nor cared for corn-flowers wild,
    Nor sung with the singing bird.

I take my heart in my hand,
    O my God, O my God,
My broken heart in my hand,
    Thou hast seen, judge thou.
My hope was written on sand,
    O my God, O my God:
Now let thy judgement stand—
    Yea, judge me now.

This contemned of a man,
    This marred one heedless day,
This heart take thou to scan
    Both within and without:
Refine with fire its gold,
    Purge thou its dross away—
Yea, hold it in thy hold,
    Whence none can pluck it out.

CHRISTINA GEORGINA ROSSETTI

I take my heart in my hand—
  I shall not die, but live—
Before thy face I stand;
  I, for thou callest such:
All that I have I bring,
  All that I am I give,
Smile thou and I shall sing,
  But shall not question much.

THOMAS HARDY
1840-1928

On the Departure Platform

We kissed at the barrier; and passing through
She left me, and moment by moment got
Smaller and smaller, until to my view
    She was but a spot;

A wee white spot of muslin fluff
That down the diminishing platform bore
Through hustling crowds of gentle and rough
    To the carriage door.

Under the lamplight's fitful glowers,
Behind dark groups from far and near,
Whose interests were apart from ours,
    She would disappear,

Then show again, till I ceased to see
That flexible form, that nebulous white;
And she who was more than my life to me
    Had vanished quite.

We have penned new plans since that fair fond day,
And in season she will appear again—
Perhaps in the same soft white array—
    But never as then!

—'And why, young man, must eternally fly
A joy you'll repeat, if you love her well?'
—O friend, nought happens twice thus; why,
    I cannot tell!

A Church Romance

(Mellstock: circa 1835)

She turned in the high pew, until her sight
Swept the west gallery, and caught its row
Of music-men with viol, book, and bow
Against the sinking sad tower-window light.

She turned again; and in her pride's depite
One strenuous viol's inspirer seemed to throw
A message from his string to her below,
Which said: 'I claim thee as my own forthright!'

Thus their hearts' bond began, in due time signed.
And long years thence, when Age had scared Romance,
At some old attitude of his or glance
That gallery-scene would break upon her mind,
With him as minstrel, ardent, young, and trim,
Bowing 'New Sabbath' or 'Mount Ephraim.'

After the Visit

    Come again to the place
Where your presence was as a leaf that skims
Down a drouthy way whose ascent bedims
    The bloom on the farer's face.

Come gain, with the feet
That were light on the green as a thistledown ball,
And those mute ministrations to one and to all
   Beyond a man's saying sweet.

   Until then the faint scent
Of the bordering flowers swam unheeded away,
And I marked not the charm in the changes of day
   As the cloud-colours came and went.

   Through the dark corridors
Your walk was so soundless I did not know
Your form from a phantom's of long ago
   Said to pass on the ancient floors,

   Till you drew from the shade,
And I saw the large luminous living eyes
Regard me in fixed inquiring-wise
   As those of a soul that weighed,

   Scarce consciously,
The eternal question of what Life was,
And why we were there, and by whose strange laws
   That which mattered most could not be.

GERARD MANLEY HOPKINS
1844-1889

Pied Beauty

Glory be to God for dappled things—
   For skies of couple-colour as a brinded cow;
      For rose-moles all in stipple upon trout that swim;
Fresh-firecoal chestnut-falls; finches' wings;
   Landscape plotted and pieced—fold, fallow, and plough;
      And áll trádes, their gear and tackle and trim.

All things counter, original, spare, strange;
   Whatever is fickle, freckled (who knows how?)
      With swift, slow; sweet, sour; adazzle, dim;
He fathers-forth whose beauty is past change:
      Praise him.

ALICE MEYNELL
1847-1922

Renouncement

I must not think of thee; and, tired yet strong,
   I shun the thought that lurks in all delight—
   The thought of thee—and in the blue Heaven's height,
And in the sweetest passage of a song.
O just beyond the fairest thoughts that throng
   This breast, the thought of thee waits hidden yet bright;
   But it must never, never come in sight;
I must stop short of thee the whole day long.
But when sleep comes to close each difficult day,
   When night gives pause to the long watch I keep,
   And all my bonds I needs must loose apart,
Must doff my will as raiment laid away,—
   With the first dream that comes with the first sleep
   I run, I run, I am gathered to thy heart.

ROBERT BRIDGES
1844-1930

My delight and thy delight

My delight and thy delight
Walking, like two angels white,
In the gardens of the night:

My desire and thy desire
Twining to a tongue of fire,
Leaping live, and laughing higher;
Thro' the everlasting strife
In the mystery of life.

Love, from whom the world begun,
Hath the secret of the sun.

Love can tell, and love alone,
Whence the million stars were strewn,
Why each atom knows its own,
How, in spite of woe and death,
Gay is life, and sweet is breath:

This he taught us, this we knew,
Happy in his science true,
Hand in hand as we stood
Neath the shadows of the wood.
Heart to heart as we lay
In the dawning of the day.

ALFRED EDWARD HOUSMAN
1859-1936

'Is My Team Ploughing?'

'Is my team ploughing,
　　That I was used to drive
And hear the harness jingle
　　When I was man alive?'

Ay, the horses trample,
　　The harness jingles now;
No change though you lie under
　　The land you used to plough.

'Is football playing
　　Along the river shore,
With lads to chase the leather,
　　Now I stand up no more?'

Ay, the ball is flying,
　　The lads play heart and soul,
The goal stands up, the keeper
　　Stands up to keep the goal.

'Is my girl happy,
　　That I thought hard to leave,
And has she tired of weeping
　　As she lies down at eve?'

ALFRED EDWARD HOUSMAN

Ay, she lies down lightly,
    She lies not down to weep:
Your girl is well contented.
    Be still, my lad, and sleep.

'Is my friend hearty,
    Now I am thin and pine,
And has he found to sleep in
    A better bed than mine?'

Yes, lad, I lie easy,
    I lie as lads would choose;
I cheer a dead man's sweetheart,
    Never ask me whose.

CLASSIC ENGLISH LOVE POEMS

BIOGRAPHIES

Robert Mannyng (or Robert de Brunne) 1288-1338. Chronicler and poet. He represented the national sentiment under the Plantagenets, introducing French words of the Midland dialect from early to later Middle English.

Geoffrey Chaucer ?1343-1400. Born in London. Page to the wife of Lionel, Duke of Clarence (1357). Served in campaign in France (1359), was captured, ransomed (1360); m. Philippa Roet (1366), sister of John of Gaunt's third wife; employed for ten years on diplomatic missions to Italy, Flanders, France, Lombardy, and met Boccaccio. Fell into poverty during the absence of his patron, John of Gaunt, and twice robbed (1390) by highwaymen. Pensions came from Richard II and Henry IV (1394, 1399). Buried in the Poets' Corner in Westminster Abbey. *The Canterbury Tales,* the stories of pilgrims assembled at the Tabard Inn in Southwark that are unfolded on the journey to Canterbury is a tableau of the fourteenth century.

Charles of Orléans ?1394-1465. Brought up at the court of Blois; as duke of Orleans he was joint commander at the battle of Agincourt (1415); taken prisoner, he was kept in England for nearly 25 years; ransomed (1440); returned to France; m. (1441) Mary of Cleves as third wife; the court at Blois was the resort of poets, including Villon; author of rondels, especially about love. He was the father of Louis XII of France.

Sir Thomas Wyatt c. 1503-1542. Diplomat, privy councilor (1533); a lover of Anne Boleyn. Henry VIII sent him on diplomatic missions; imprisoned as an ally of the earl of Essex (1541); translator of Petrarchan sonnets, and pioneered the sonnet in England; contributed sonnets, rondeaux, satire in heroic couplets, and lyric poems.

John Lyly ?1544-1606. Born in Kent; M.A. at Oxford (1575); studied at Cambridge; known chiefly for his didactic romance in two parts, *Euphues, the Anatomy of Wit* (1579) and *Euphues and his England* (1580) aiming at education, manners, and eschewing the affected style that was ridiculed by Shakespeare. As a dramatist he introdcued English high comedy and made prose its vehicle.

William Shakespeare 1564-1616. Born in Stratford Upon Avon (records show 44 different spellings of the surname). Dramatist and poet, he was the son of John Shakespeare, a glover and dealer in farm produce; m. Anne Hathaway (1582). Established in London as actor-playwright (1592); member of the chamberlain's players, (formed 1594; became king's players 1603.) Prospered financially; a grant of the family arms made to his father (1596); purchased (1597) New Place in Stratford and acquired other property there; continued to live chiefly in London. The dates of plays are still conjectural; the last work, *The Two Noble Kinsmen*, in collaboration (1613). The *Sonnets* (pub. 1609).

Ben Jonson ?1573-1637. Playwright and poet, born in Westminster. He studied in Westminster school, and perhaps in Cambridge. Served briefly with the English army in Flanders; returned to London (c. 1592) and became associated with the stage, as both playwright and actor. His plays include *Volpone, Bartholomew Fair, The Devil's an Ass, Epicoene* between 1605 and 1616. Among his poems (pub. 1616) were epigrams, epistles and songs, including the famous *Drink to me only with thine eyes*. He is regarded as the first poet laureate in the English language, although he bears no official title.

Christopher Marlowe 1564-1593. Dramatist. Born in Canterbury, son of a shoemaker. M.A. Canterbury (1587); he attached himself early as a dramatist to the Admiral's Men, the earl of Nottingham's theatrical company which produced most of Marlowe plays; *Tamburlaine the Great* (acted in 1587 or 1588, pub. 1590); first dramatist to discover the vigor and variety of blank verse; wrote *The Tragedy of Dr. Faustus* (1601); produced *The Jew of Malta* after 1588; pub. 1633. Credited on internal evidence, *Titus Andronicus* of Shakespeare suggests Marlowe's hand in the authorship. Credited also with the second and third parts of *Henry VI*, completed and revised by Shakespeare; author of short poems, including *Come live with me and be my love* (to which Ralegh wrote a reply, *If all the world and love were young*). Marlowe was denounced for propagating atheistical opinions; he was killed in a tavern brawl.

Sir Walter Ralegh ?1552-1618. He spelled his name consistently, from 1581, and never Raleigh, the prevailing modern form. Courtier, navigator, historian, and poet. Engaged in piratical expeditions against the Spaniards (1578); active in the suppression of Munster (1580). At court as a protege of Leicester, and caught Queen Elizabeth's fancy; given estates, license for exporting woolen goods and made warden of the stannaries. Granted a patent to unknown lands in America in the queen's name; sent on an expedition which explored the coast north of Florida to North Carolina (1584) and named the coast north of Florida, "Virginia" for Elizabeth the virgin queen. He sent settlers (1585) to Roanoke Island, North Carolina, but the settlers deserted the colony (1586); later made unsuccessful attempts to colonize Virginia. He succeeded introducing potatoes and tobacco into England, also in Ireland, where he set about repeopling his estates, and where he became a friend of the poet Spenser; eclipsed as the favorite by Essex and was banished for four years from the queen's presence because of intrigue of a secret marriage with one of her maids, Elizabeth Throckmorton. He fitted out bootless expeditions to seek what was supposed about Guiana, explored the coasts of Trinidad and sailed the Orinoco (1595); took a brilliant part in an expedition against Cadiz (1596) and an attack on the Azores (1597). On the death of Queen Elizabeth (1603) he was stripped of his offices; on a charge of conspiring against James I, he was sent to the Tower of London where he lived with wife and son (1616) and composed his *History of* *the World* (1614; carried down to 130 B.C.). Released to seek gold along the Orinoco, under promise not to entrench on the Spanish; lost his fleet by storms, lost men by desertion and disease, stricken with fever, lost his son Walter, and returned (1618). On the demand of the Spanish minister, angered over the destruction of the new Spanish town, San Tomas, he was beheaded at Whitehall under the old sentence against him. Author of poems, of which only about thirty fragments survive, including *Cynthia, the lady of the sea; Methought I saw the grave where Laura lay; The lie; The Pilgrimage;* prose work on the fight over the Azores and the discovery of Guiana; and political essays.

John Donne 1573-1631. Chief of the metaphysical poets; born in London, son of a wealthy ironmonger. Brought up as Roman Catholic; studied law; joined the Anglican church. Sailed in Essex's expedition to Cadiz (1596); dismissed from private secretaryship to Sir Thomas Egerton, keeper of the great seal, because of the clandestine marriage with his patron's niece. Published an extravagant elegy on the daughter of his host, Sir Robert Drury, *An Anatomy of the World* (1611); contended in *Biathanatos* (pub. 1644) that suicide was essentially sinful. Having won approval of James I with *Pseudo-Martyr* (1610), assuring Roman Catholics of freedom from inconsistency in taking an oath of allegiance to James I, and followed the king's suggestion that he take holy orders (1614); he preached sermons unexcelled in the 17th century; executed a mission to Bohemia and preached before Princess Elizabeth at Heidelberg (1619); was dean of St. Paul's (1621-31); preached often before Charles I. Among his poetical works are *Of the Progress of the Soul* (begun 1601; pub. 1633; a satire setting up a hypothetical metempsychosis of the soul), *Divine Poems* (1607), *Epithalamium* (1613), the marriage of count palatine and the Princess Elizabeth; *Cycle of Holy Sonnets* (1618). Izaak Walton wrote a biography of his friend.

Michael Drayton 1563-1631. Born in Warwickshire. Settled in London (1590). His earliest volume of poems, The Harmony of the Church (1591), was burned by public order. Pulished a volume of eclogues, Idea: The Shepard's Garland (1593); a cycle of 64 sonnets in honor of Warwickshire lady; three historical poems, Piers Gaveston (1593, Matilda (1594), Robert, Duke of Normandy (1596). The Baron's Wars; collaborated in dramatic work with Henry Chettle, Thomas Decker, and John Webster; included in Poems Lyrical and Pastoral (c. 1605) the spirited Ballad of Agincourt. Finished his magnum opus, Polybion (1622), a topographical description of England in twelve-syllabled verse; published miscellaneous volume (1627), including his most graceful poem, Nymphidia (an epic of fairyland), and The Battle of Agincourt (a historical poem in ottava rima), not to be confused with the ballad; his last work, The Muses Elyzium (1630), contain pastorals.

Thomas Ford. d. 1648. *There is a lady sweet and kind* is usually sung in three quatrains. The second quatrain begins: *Her gesture, motion and her smiles*; the third quatrain begins: *Cupid is winged and doth range.*
The remaining three quatrains appear to be the work of an intruder; he shows his wit more than his love.

George Wither 1588-1667. Poet and pamphleteer. Imprisoned in the Marshalsea for satire, *Abuses Stript and Whipped* (1613), said to be libelous; during imprisonment wrote pastoral, *Shephard's Hunting* (1615), said to be libelous.

Robert Herrick 1591-1674. Lyric poet; vicar of Dean Prior in Devonshire (1629-47; 1662-74); ejected for Royalist sympathies (1647); restored (1662). Published his collected verse, *Hesperides, or the Works both human and Divine of Robert Herrick, Esq. 1648).*

Edmund Waller 1606-1687. Adressed verses to Sacharissa, that is, Lady Dorothy Sidney; conducted (1641) impeachment of Sir Francis Crawley, judge in common pleas, for maintaining (1636) the legality of ship money; detected in a plot, known as "Waller's Plot," for seizing London for Charles I (1643); spared death on betrayal of his associates; expelled from the House of Commons, fined ten thousand pounds, and banished (1644). Permitted to return (1652), wrote a panegyric of Cromwell (1655) and a poem of rejoicing on his death (1659). On the Restoration wrote eulogy of Charles II; M.P. (1661-87) and favorite at court. Author of *Poems* (1645), elegant and graceful but rather frigid and artificial, *St. James's Park* (1661), and *Divine Poems* (1685); he made the heroic couplet fashionable.

Andrew Marvell 1621-1678. Poet and satirist. Tutor to the daughter of Lord Fairfax (c. 1650); wrote poems on gardens and country life, *Horatian Ode upon Cromwell's Return from Ireland* (1650); Milton's colleague in Latin secretaryship (1657); M.P. (1660) with republic leanings, but favorite of Charles II. As a political writer, vigorously opposed government after the Restoration in pamphlets and satires, as the *Growth of Popery and Arbitrary Government in England* (1677); defended Milton; turned satire on Charles II (c. 1672) and monarchy, endangering his life. Author of a few poems of high poetic quality, as *The Emigrants in the Bermudas, The Nymph Complaining for the Death of My Fawn, Thoughts in a Garden, To His Coy Mistress.*

Thomas Stanley 1625-1678. Classical scholar; descendant of 3d earl of Derby; M.A. Canterbury (1641); published translations of Tasso, Petrarch, Lope de Vega, and Greek and Latin poets; author of *History of Philosophy* (4 vols., 1655-62) edited Aeschylus with Latin translation and commentary (1663-64).

John Wilmot 1647-1680. 2d earl, poet, became a favorite courtier and boon companion of Charles II, and one of the most dissolute; patron of several poets; repented on his deathbed, according to a popular pamphlet by Bishop Burnet; author of graceful amorous lyrics, mordant satires in verse, and a tragedy, *Valentinian* (produced 1685), adapted from Beaumont and Fletcher.

Aphra Behn, nee Johnson. 1640-1689. Dramatist and novelist. Lived from childhood (to 1658) in Surinam, West Indies; met Oroonoko, "the royal slave"; m. merchant named Behn (d. 1666); served as a spy in Antwerp, unrewarded; imprisoned for debt. First English woman professional writer; author of vivacious, rather coarse comedies, including *Forc'd Marriage* (1671), *The Rover* (1677), *False Count* (1682), a satrical play, *The Roundheads*, attacking Puritans, of poems and translations, of novels and tales, including *Oroonoke* (c. 1678).

John Dryden 1631-1700. Poet, born in Northamptonshire. Clerk to his cousin Sir Gilbert Pickering, Cromwell's chamberlain; panagyrist in *Heroic Stanzas on the Death of Oliver Cromwell* (pub. with two poems by Thomas Sprat and Edmund Waller, 1659) and panagyric on the Restoration (1661); m. (1663) Lady Elizabeth Howard, sister of his patron. Established reputation with *The Rival Ladies* (1663, a tragicomedy using the rhymed couplet); *Marriage-a-la-Mode* (his best comedy, 1673), *Aurengzebe* (a rhymed tragedy, 1676), *All for Love* (a version of the story of Antony and Cleopatra in blank verse, 1678) and *The Spanish Fryar* (1681), besides adaptations of Shakespeare's tragedies. Published *Annus Mirabilis*, treating of the great fire and the Dutch war (1667). Poet laureate and historiographer (1670). He was beaten by masked bravoes of John Wilmot, Earl of Rochester, for an attributed derogatory passage in an anonymous essay (1679). Partly in retaliation for Buckingham's ridicule of heroic in *The Rehearsal*, and launched in *Absalom and Achitofel* (1681), a crushing satire upon Monmouth, Shaftsbury, Buckingham, Charles II and others involved to exclude the Duke of York in favor of the Duke of Monmouth. Dryden defended Anglicanism in *Religio Laici* (1682). Declining to take oaths at the English Revolution, he lost his places and pensions (1689). *Fables, Ancient and Modern* (1699) was his last great work.

Sir Charles Sedley ?1639-1701. A wit and dramatist of the Restoration; notarious man of fashion and profligate; known for his bon mots; author of two tragedies, *Antony and Cleopatra* (1677) and *The Tyrant King of Crete* (1702), three comedies including *Bellamira* (1687), society verse, and songs, including *Phyllis Is My Only Joy.*

Matthew Prior, often called Matt 1664-1721. Diplomat and poet; friend of Charles Montagu (afterwards the earl of Halifax), with whom he wrote (1687) *The City Mouse and the Country Mouse* in ridicule of Dryden's *Hind and the Panther*; secretary to the ambassador at the Hague; secretary in negotiations at Rijwijk (1697); went over to the Tories (1702). Employed through Queen Anne's reign in negotiations with France; took the leading part framing the Treaty of Utrecht (1713), called "Matt's Peace"; on Queen Anne's death he was impeached by Sir Robert Walpole and imprisoned (1717). In prison he composed a long humorous poem, *Alma, or the Progress of the Mind* (1718). Known for his neat epigrams; for elegance and easy grace of his familiar verse, as in *To a Child of Quality* and *The Female Phaeton.*

Alexander Pope 1688-1744. Son of a Roman Catholic linen draper; developed a physical deformity as a result of severe illness at the age of twelve; undermined his health by overstudy. Attracted Whycherley's attention to his verse (1704); Addison's praise for the *Essay on Criticism* (1711) and wide and sure reputation with a brilliant mock-heroic poem, *The Rape of the Lock* (1712); gained friendship of Swift with *Windsor Forest* (1713); with Swift and Arbuthnot they formed the Scriblerus Club (1741); earned independence with his translations of the *Iliad* (1715-20) and the *Odyssey* (1725-26); moved (1719) with his mother to a villa at Twickenham. Jointly with Swift published *Miscellanies* (1727-32), parodies upon writers, which evoked a storm of abusive and scurrilous retorts from those who thought themselves injured; he answered these in the famous lampoon, the *Dunciad* (1728, 1742), keen and biting satire on dullness in general and on particular poetasters. Under the influence of his friend Lord Bolingbroke, attempted a systematic, complete *Essay on Man* (1733), lines and couplets which are household quotations still. In his last works, *Imitations of Horace* (1733-39) became the mouthpiece of his political friends in satirizing Walpole's adherents, indulging savage vindictiveness, as the attack upon the former friend Lady Mary Wortley Montagu and offer gross insult to Lord Hervey.

Lady Mary Wortley Montagu 1689-1762. Poet and letter writer; daughter of Evelyn Pierrepont, 1st Duke of Kingston; precocious child, taught herself Latin, clever and witty in presiding at her father's table. She accompanied her husband on an embassy to Constantinople (1716-18), whence she wrote sparkling *Letters from the East*, on her return she introduced inoculation for smallpox, which she had observed in Turkey. She settled in Twickenham, leader of society and fashion, and renewed her friendship with Pope and Swift. Quarreled with Pope (1722); bitterly attacked by Pope and Swift; left her husband and her country to live in Italy (1739-69) whence she wrote letters to her daughter, Countess of Bute. Author of *Town Eclogues* (1716).

Walter Savage Landor 1775-1864. Poet and prose writer, born in Warwick; removed from Rubgy for insubordination and intractable temper; rusticated from Oxford (1794); quarreled with his family; retired to South Wales on an allowance. Gained friendship with Southey; went through his fortune; fought as a volunteer in Spain (1808). Bought Llanthony Abbey, Monmouthshire, but quarreled with his neighbors and tenants; m. Thuillier (1811); lived successively in France, at Como, and at Florence; Quarreled with his wife and returned (1835). Returned to Florence (1858) because of a libel action; assisted by Robert Browning. Author of a tragedy, *Don Julian* (1812), *Imaginary Conversations* (five vols. 1824, 1828, 1829), *The Examination of William Shakespeare...Touching Deer-Stealing* (1834), *Hellenics* (1847), *Poemata et Inscriptiones* (1847), and *Dry Sticks, Fagoted* (1858). Caricatured as Lawrence Boythorn in *Dickens's Bleak House*.

John Keats 1795-1821. Son of a London hostler. Studied medicine but never practiced. His first-published verse a sonnet in Leigh Hunt's *Examiner* (May 5, 1816), followed by sonnet *On First Looking into Chapman's Homer* (Dec. 1816), and other sonnets (1817); with the aid of Shelley, published *Poems by John Keats* (March, 1817). Wrote *Endymion* (April-December, 1817); finished *The Eve of St. Agnes* (1819) and *La Belle Dame sans Merci* (1819). Fell in love with Fanny Brawne. Published *Lamia and Other Poems* (July, 1820). For his health Keats went to Italy; died in Rome (February 23, 1821). His *Hyperion* (begun in 1818) remained unfinished at his death.

Thomas Hood 1799-1845. Poet and humorist, born in London. Son of Thomas Hood (d. 1811), Scottish bookseller. Learned engraving; subeditor, *London Magazine* (1821-23); showed poetical powers as editor (1829) of the *Gem*, an annual in which appeared *Eugene Aram's Dream* (1829); wrote other serious verse, including *The Bridge of Sighs* (1844); began *Hood's Magazine* (1844); his *Song of the Shirt* appeared in *Punch* (1843).

Percy Bysshe Shelley 1792-1822. Poet, born in Warnham, near Horsham, Sussex; educ. Eton and University College, Oxford, where he was expelled, with his friend Thomas Jefferson Hogg, for circulating pamphlet, *The Necessity of Atheism* (1811); m. Harriet Westbrook, daughter of a retired inkeeper (1811); filled with revolutionary ardor, visited Ireland and addressed the Dublin assembly held by O'Connell; driven from Tanyrallt, Wales, by a supposed attempt on his life. Became a disciple of the philosophical radical William Godwin; abandoned Harriet (later making a settlement on her) and eloped to Switzerland with Godwin's daughter, Mary (see Mary Wollstonecraft Shelley), whom he married (1816) after Harriet's suicide; refused custody of his two children by decision of Lord Eldon on the ground of his atheism and not fit to raise children; visited Byron in Switzerland (1816). After a pulmonary attack, left England never to return. He spent the rest of his life in company with Byron, Edward Trelawny, and an ex-officer, Edward Williams, in Italy (1818-19) at Byron's villa near Este, and in Venice, Rome, Leghorn, and Florence; settled in Pisa (1820); worked on his last poems at Lerici on the Gulf of Spezia (1822); visited Leigh Hunt at Pisa and was lost in a storm while sailing back with Edward Williams; his body, washed ashore, was burnt on a pyre. *Ode to the West Wind* (1819), *The Skylark* (1820), *Epipsychidion* (in homage to ideal womanhood; completed after meeting a young Italian noblewoman, Emilia Viviani), *Adonais* (on the death of Keats) are specimens of Shelley's last poems; *The Defense of Poetry*, in prose, was in answer to Peacock.

George Gordon Noel, Lord Byron. 1788-1824. Born in London; lived with his mother at Aberdeen until on the death of his great uncle (1798); he succeeded to the barony created for an ancestor John (d. 1552); educ. Harrow and Trinity College, Cambridge, where he published (1807) a volume of poems, *Hours of Idleness*, which was fiercely assailed by the *Edinburgh Review*; he replied in a witty satirical poem, *English Bards and Scotch Reviewers* (1809). Traveled in Portugal, Spain, Greece, Turkey, swimming the Hellespont (May 3, 1810); addressed *Maid of Athens* to Theresa Macri, his hostess's daughter; spoke twice in the House of Lords (1812); gained fame with publication of the first two cantos of *Childe Harold's Pilgrimage*, a narrative poem of travels through Southern Europe by an imaginary pilgrim (1812). Published (1813-14) Turkish tales in verse, *The Giaour, The Bride of Abdos, The Corsair, Lara*, which were as popular as *Childe Harold*. m. (January 1815) Anne Isabella Milbanke (1792-1860), a mathematician and heiress who gave birth (1815) to Augusta Ada, and returned to her father's protection (January 1816) and became Baroness Wentworth (1856). Byron signed the deed of separation from his wife and left England (1816) never to return; traveled in Switzerland with Shelley; wrote *Childe Harold*, canto iii (1816) and *The Prisoner of Chillon* (1816); lived at or near Venice (1816-1819); had a child, Allegra, by Jane Clairmont (1817); finished canto iv of *Childe Harold* and began (1818) *Don Juan,* a satirical epic poem, narrating the adventures of a libertine. Took Teresa, Countess Guicciolli, from her husband (1819). Joined Leigh Hunt in *The Liberal* magazine (1822) in which he took revenge upon Southey with *The Vision of Judgment*; was present at the cremation of Shelley (1822); in the *Prophecy of Dante* (1821) denounced tyranny and spoke out as a champion of liberty for the oppressed in Italy. He adapted a German tale as *Werner* (1822), a successful play with Macready in the leading part; after the death of his daughter Allegra he composed his last play, *The Deformed Transformed* (1824); after *The Island* (1823), based on Bligh's account of mutiny on the *Bounty*, he continued *Don Juan*; accepted the invitation of Prince Mavrokordatos to join the Greek insurgents in the struggle for independence, enlisted a regiment, advanced large sums; died at Missolonghi of malaria.

William Blake 1757-1827. Artist, poet, and mystic. Apprenticed to an engraver (1771-78); used new process of printing from etched copper plates in a series of his own lyrical poems, hand-illustrated and colored, beginning with *Songs of Innocence* (1789) and *Songs of Experience* (1794), the last name including *Tiger! Tiger! burning bright.* Illustrated Mary Wollstonecraft's works (1791) and Young's *Night Thouts* (1793-1800). Executed and engraved many religious designs, his best *Inventions to the Book of Job* (1820-26; occupied at the time of his death in engraving signs for Dante's *Divina Commedia*. Author of mystical and metaphysical works in *Prophetic Books* (1793-1804), and symbolic poems terminating with *Milton* (1804) and *Jerusalem* (1804-18).

George Crabbe 1754-1832. Born Aldeburgh, Suffolk, where he practiced surgery. Published first poem, *Inebriety*, in Ipswich (1775), *The Candidate*, in London (1780); befriended by Edmund Burke, who helped him with the publication of *The Library* (1781) and *The Village* (1783) and in entering the church and obtaining livings in Dorsetshire. Published *The Parish Register* (1807), *The Borough* (1810), *Tales in Verse* (1812), and *Tales of the Hall* (1819).

BIOGRAPHIES

William Wordsworth 1770-1850. Born in Cockermouth, Cumberland. B.A. Canerbury (1791); traveled in France (1792); sympathized with French revolutionary spirit; fell in love with a surgeon's daughter, Marie Anne ("Annette") Vallon, who bore him a daughter, Anne Caroline (b. 1792); m. Jean Baptiste Martin Baudouin (1816), an episode reflected in *Vaudracour and Julia*. Published (1793) first works, *The Evening Walk* and *Descriptive Sketches*, the latter an account of a walking tour in the Alps; began (1793) *Guilt and Sorrows*; in a period of pessimism wrote (1795-96) a tragedy, *The Borderers*. On receipt of nine hundred pounds legacy settled with his sister Dorothy at Racedown, Dorsetshire; moved to Alfoxden, Somerset, to be near Samuel Taylor Coleridge, with whom he wrote *Lyrical Ballads* (1798, 1800, 1802, 1805) a collection of poems representing the revolt against the artificial style; increased the hostility of the critics by the statement of his poetical principles and his theory of poetic diction. Lived (1798-??) in Goslar, Germany, where he began *The Prelude* (completed 1805), published after his death. Settled (1799) at Grasmere with Dorothy; m. Mary Hutchinson (b. 1770), after the revelation of the story of Annette. Became an opponent of liberalism; made tours in Scotland (1801, 1803) and began a friendship with Walter Scott (1803); after a tour in Scotland he pulished *Yarrow Visited* and turned to classical subjects. After his last visit to Scott at Abbotsford he wrote *Yarrow Revisited*; some of his splendid sonnets were written in a period of declining power; succeeded Southey as poet laureate (1843); buried in Grasmere churchyard.

John Clare 1793-1864. Known as the Northhampshire peasant poet. Herd boy, gardener, militiaman, lime burner, vagrant; published *Poems Descriptive of Rural Life and Scenery* (1820); failed as a farmer (1827, 1831); confined in a lunatic asylum; profited little by other poetic works, *Village Minstrel* (1821), *The Shepards Calendar* (1827), *Rural Muse* (1835).

Elizabeth Barrett Browning 1806-1861. Read Homer in Greek at eight; translated *Prometheus Bound* (1833); wrote many original poems. While saddling a horse at fifteen she injured her spine, and she was a semi-invalid for many years; regained strength some time previous to her marriage (1846) to Robert Browning but was always delicate; she expressed her hesitation to burden him with an invalid wife in *Sonnets from the Portuguese*, written in secret, first seen by Robert Browning, and published in 1850. She sympathized with the struggle of the Florentines for freedom in *Casa Guidi Windows* (1851). She completed *Aurora Leigh* (1856), expressing her "highest convictions in work and art." She was bitterly disappointed by the peace of Villafranca. Her last work was *Poems before Congress* (1860).

Robert Browning 1812-1889. Son of clerk in the Bank of England, having literary and artistic tastes, and a mother having a passion for music. Showed Shelleyan influence in his first published work, *Pauline* (anonymously 1833). Wrote earliest of his dramatic lyrics, *Porphyria's Lover* (1834), in Russia; published long dramatic poems *Paracelsus* (1835) and *Sordello* (1840). Urged by Macready, wrote tragedy, *Strafford*, produced at Covent Garden (1837), followed by other plays, including *Pippa Passes, Return of the Druses, Blot in the 'Scutcheon, Columbe's Birthday*. Contributed to *Hood's Magazine* (1844-45) *The Bishop Ordered His Tomb*. m. (1846) Elizabeth Barrett and lived for the next fifteen years more or less in seclusion, mainly in Italy; published *Christmas Eve*, and *Easter Day* (1850) and *Men and Women* (1855, including *Fra Lippo Lippi*); returned to London upon his wife's death (1861), and in psychological monologues of *Dramatis Personae* (1864, including *Prospice, Rabbi Ben Ezra, A Death in the Desert, Caliban upon Setebos*) found his best form; wrote *The Ring and the Book* (1864-69), often regarded as Browning's masterpiece. *Asolando*, 1889, appeared the day of his death. Buried in Westminster Abbey.

Alfred, Lord Tennyson 1809-1892. Born at Somersby, Lincolnshire, four of eight sons. Published with his brother Charles *Poems by Two*

Brothers (1827); at Trinity College, Cambridge, one of a gifted group known as "The Apostles." Won the chancellor's poem *Timbuctoo* (1829) in blank verse and published *Poems Chiefly Lyrical* (1830). Left Cambridge without a degree (February 1831); traveled with Arthur Henry Hallam in the Pyrenees and on the Rhine (1832); met with scant success of *Poems* (1832), including *The Lady of Shallott, The Palace of Art, The Lotus Eaters, A Dream of Fair Women,* brutally reviewed by Lockhart in the *Quarterly Review.* On the death of Hallam, his sister's fiancee, wrote *Two Voices* and began *In Memoriam.* Spent nine years reading and meditating before *Poems* (2 vols., 1842: including *Morte D'Arthur, Ulysses, Locksley Hall, Godiva,* and *Break, Break, Break*), which secured his place as a great poet. In the eventful year of 1850 published *In Memoriam,* one of the great elegies, married Emily Sellwood, and was appointed poet laureate on the death of Wordsworth. Traveled in Italy, settled at Twickenham, wrote *Ode* on the death of Wellington. Moved to Farringford on the Isle of Wight (1853) where he lived part of each year for the rest of his life. Wrote *The Charge of the Light Brigade* (1854); puzzled the public with *Maud* (1855); awakened the public with the *Idylls of the King* (1859); added to, 1869, 1872; completed, 1885; turned to a series of historical dramas, *Queen Mary* (1875), *Harold* (1876), *Becket* (1884). Built Aldworth, his second residence, near Haslemere (1868-70); raised to the peerage as Baron Tennyson of Freshwater and Aldworth. Showed active imagination during his last years in *The Revenge, Defence of Lucknow,* and other ballads; buried in Westminster Abbey.

Emily Bronte 1818-1848. Charlotte (1816-1855), Emily Jane, and Anne (1820-1849) were novelists. Emily wrote one novel only, *Wuthering Heights,* a story of passion. Charlotte Bronte wrote *Jane Eyre* (1847). Anne Bronte produced *Agnes Grey* and *The Tenant of Wildfell Hall.* All of the sisters wrote verse as well.

Matthew Arnold 1822-1888. Poet and critic. Grad. Balliol, Oxford (1844); Newdigate prizeman (1843). Inspector of schools (1851-86).

Professor of Poetry, Oxford (1857-67). Lectured in America (1883-84, 1886). His poetic works included *The Strayed Reveller and Other Poems* (1849), *Empedocles on Etna and Other Poems, The Scholar Gypsy;* Critical essays include *On Translating Homer,* two series of *Essays in Criticism* (1865-, 1888), *Culture and Anarchy* (1869), *Literature and Dogma* (1873).

Christina Georgina Rossetti 1830-1894. Lived all her life in London. Contributed seven lyric poems to *The Germ* under the pseudonym of Ellen Alleyne (1850); model to her brother, Dante Gabriel Rossetti, the poet and painter; also to Holman Hunt, Ford Madox Brown, and Millais; published her best verse in *Goblin Market* (1862); afflicted with Graves disease (1871); from religious scruples she twice declined proposals of marriage; long attended her mother and devoted herself to religious disquisition. Author of *The Face of the Deep* (a commentary on the Apocalypse (1892), besides further poetical works, *The Prince's Progress* (1866), *A Pageant* (1881), *New Poems* (1896).

Thomas Hardy 1840-1928. Born in Dorsetshire. Studied architecture but devoted himself to literature (from 1867); Order of Merit (1911). Among his many novels, *Far From the Madding Crowd* (1874), *The Return of the Native* (1878), *The Mayor of Casterbridge* (1886), *Tess of the D'Urbervilles* (1891), *Jude the Obscure* (1895). Among his poetical works are the *Wessex Poems* (1898), *Poems of the Past and Present* (1901), *The Dynasts* (a poetic drama in three parts (1904-08).

Gerard Manley Hopkins 1844-1889. A Jesuit priest and poet. His poems, posthumously, include *The Wreck of the Deutschland, The Windhover,* and *Vision of the Mermaid.*

Alice Meynell 1847-1922. Published her first poems, *Preludes* (1875), praised by Ruskin, Rossetti, and Browning; aided her husband in editing the Catholic periodical *Weekly Register* (1881-98) and *Merry England* (1883-95), through which the Meynells discovered and aided

Francis Thompson the poet; gained literary fame with the publication of a volume of prose essays, *The Rhythm of Life* (1893); published anthologies and a life of Ruskin (1900), also in *A Father of Women* (1917), and essays in *Hearts of Controversy* (1917).

Robert Bridges 1844-1930. Poet laureate (1913-30). Practiced medicine in hospitals (1875-82). Lived in Berkshire, pursuing poetry and music (until 1904); here he wrote one long narrative poem, *Eros and Psyche* (1885), and eight dramas. Engaged in metrical experimentation and inaugurated, in pamphlet *On Prosody of Paradise Regained and Samson Agonistes* (1889), new development in English verse, giving freedom to natural accentuation and allowing fresh flexibility of rhythm. Published *The Spirit of Man* (1916), a prose and verse anthology "designed to bring fortitude" and war poems collected in *October* (1920). His magnum opus, *The Testament of Beauty* (begun 1926, published 1929), summing up his aesthetic and spiritual experience. His prose works include *Milton's Prosody* (1893), John Keats, a *Critical Essay* (1895).

Alfred Edward Housman 1859-1936. Classical scholar and poet; educ. Oxford. Professor of Latin, University College, London (1892-1911), and Cambridge (1911-36). Edited works of Manilius, Juvenal, and Lucan. Published volumes of verse, *A Shropshire Lad* (1896) and *Last Poems* (1922). Another volume, *More Poems*, was published posthumously (1936); the definitive *Collected Poems of A.E. Housman* was published in 1940.

Love Poetry from Hippocrene . . .

CLASSIC AMERICAN LOVE POEMS

EDITED BY EMILE CAPOUYA

These verses of love express a unique American voice on the subject. This lovely anthology comes in a charmingly illustrated gift edition, with nearly 100 poems of love from 50 American poets, including Anne Bradstreet, Edna St. Vincent Millay, James Wright and Robert Lowell.

130 pages • 6 x9 • illustrations • 0-7818-0645-3 • W • $17.50hc • (731) • May

CLASSIC FRENCH LOVE POEMS

EDITED BY LISA NEAL

This lovely gift edition contains 120 inspiring love poems translated into English from French, the language of love itself, including a complete translation of Paul Géraldy's *Toi et Moi*. Also featured are 25 beautiful illustrations from famous artist Maurice Leloir.

130 pages • 6 x 9 • illustrations • 0-7818-0573-2 • W • $17.50hc • (672)

SCOTTISH LOVE POEMS: A PERSONAL ANTHOLOGY

Re-issued edition

EDITED BY LADY ANTONIA FRASER

Lady Fraser collects the loves and passions of her fellow Scots, from Burns to Aileen Campbell Nye, into a book that will find a way to touch everyone's heart.

253 pages • 5½ x 8¼ • 0-7818-0406-X • NA • $14.95pb • (482)

HEBREW LOVE POEMS

EDITED BY DAVID C. GROSS

ILLUS. BY SHRAGA WEIL

Several translators have reworked over 90 love lyrics from biblical times to current poetry written in modern Israel.

"A volume of great beauty and range." —*Booklist*

91 pages • 6 x 9 • illus. • 0-7818-0430-2 • $14.95pb • (473)

IRISH LOVE POEMS: DÁNTA GRÁ

EDITED BY PAULA REDES

ILLUS. BY PEADAR McDAID

Mingling the famous, the infamous, and the unknown into a striking collection, these works span four centuries up to the most modern of poets such as Nuala Ni Dhomhnaill and Brendan Kennelly.

146 pages • 6 x 9 • illus. • 0-7818-0396-9 • W • $17.50hc • (70)

All prices subject to change. **To purchase Hippocrene Books** contact your local bookstore, call (718) 454-2366, or write to: HIPPOCRENE BOOKS, 171 Madison Avenue, New York, NY 10016. Please enclose check or money order, adding $5.00 shipping (UPS) for the first book and $.50 for each additional book.